ZAGATSURVEY®

1999

SAN DIEGO RESTAURANTS

Edited by David Nelson

Coordinated by Myrna Marston
and Susan K. Safronoff

Published and distributed by
ZAGAT SURVEY, LLC
4 Columbus Circle
New York, New York 10019
Tel: 212 977 6000
E-mail: zagat@zagatsurvey.com
Web site: www.zagat.com

Acknowledgments

We gratefully acknowledge the assistance of the following people and organizations: Beth, Paul & Peter Safronoff, the American Institute of Wine and Food, and the *San Diego Metropolitan, Uptown Examiner & Daily Business Report.*

Contents

Starters

Here are the results of our *1999 San Diego Restaurant Survey* covering some 595 restaurants in the San Diego area.

By regularly surveying large numbers of local restaurant-goers, we think we have achieved a uniquely current and reliable guide. We hope you agree. More than 780 people participated. Since the participants dined out an average of 3.9 times per week, this *Survey* is based on about 158,000 meals per year.

We want to thank each of our participants. They are a widely diverse group in all respects but one – they are food lovers all. This book is really "theirs."

Of the surveyors, 55% are women, 45% are men; the breakdown by age is 13% in their 20s, 20% in their 30s, 21% in their 40s, 30% in their 50s and 16% in their 60s or above.

To help guide our readers to San Diego's best meals and best buys, we have prepared a number of lists. See, for example, Most Popular Restaurants (page 11), Top Ratings (pages 12–16) and Best Buys (pages 17–18). On the assumption that most people want a quick fix on the places at which they are considering eating, we have tried to be concise and to provide handy indexes.

We are particularly grateful to our editor, David Nelson, a restaurant critic for *San Diego Magazine, Westways,* and other publications, and our coordinators, Myrna Marston, who owns a public relations agency in San Diego, and Susan K. Safronoff, who has coordinated *Surveys,* including *U.S. Hotels, Resorts & Spas,* for over 12 years.

We invite you to be a reviewer in our next *Survey*. To do so, simply send a stamped, self-addressed, business-size envelope to ZAGAT SURVEY, 4 Columbus Circle, New York, NY 10019, so that we will be able to contact you. Each participant will receive a free copy of the next *San Diego Restaurant Survey* when it is published.

Your comments, suggestions and even criticisms of this *Survey* are also solicited. There is always room for improvement with your help.

New York, New York   Nina and Tim Zagat
February 17, 1999

What's New

When I moved to San Diego in 1978, it was nigh impossible to find even a decent take-out sandwich. Chief among the obstacles were dreadful, cottony bread and counter help that assumed everyone wanted avocado, cheese and mayo on their corned beef on rye. At a deli regarded as among the city's best, I once ordered an Italian grinder on a hard roll. The woman waiting on me stared mutely until finally she turned to the bin of buns, rummaged about and pulled one out from the bottom. "This is from yesterday," she said, her voice innocent of any irony. "It's probably hard enough."

Things sure have changed since those stale days. Wave after wave of talented chefs and restaurateurs from across the country and around the globe have been descending upon this lovely city of hills and canyons, of cliffs and beaches, constantly challenging our tastes and expanding our gastronomical horizons. For example, San Diegans can now find artisanal bread most everywhere, thanks to entrepreneurs like Charles Kaufman, who a few years ago opened Bread & Cie., a stunningly successful, French-style *boulangerie* in Hillcrest, stocked with an array of irresistible loaves.

SD's appeal as a sunny destination for tourists and conventioneers has also contributed to its restaurant boom, but no more so than the increasing sophistication of the city itself. Take a look at the Gaslamp Quarter. Since it emerged from a half-century of neglect and transformed itself into an enchanting historic district, its popularity has continued to rise, and today the Quarter is as sizzling as it is eclectic, with the debut of the Lobster Co., a whimsical seafood house; Morton's of Chicago, a palatial homage to prime meat; Sadaf Restaurant, an attractive, aromatic Persian; and Taka, an ultrahip Asian-Fusion. Or observe the action in trendy Hillcrest, where the kind of innovative places like Gulf Coast Grill and Mixx that now crowd its cutting-edge streets would have been unimaginable only a decade ago. All the while, stalwart locales like exclusive La Jolla continue to lure diners, especially since eateries that once merely rented tables with gorgeous views are being supplanted by establishments that take cooking seriously, such as the quaint Roma Beach Caffe and the pleasant La Bruschetta.

Along with the region's spectacular growth has come widening ethnic diversity, which has made the city one of the culinary capitals on the West Coast. The cleverly creative menus of such multicultural jewels as La Jolla's Cafe Japengo and Roppongi have helped turn San Diego's orientation away from the "I'll have a salad with blue cheese dressing, prime rib with a baked potato and cheesecake" mantra of the '80s towards our current fascination with East-meets-West fusion. While it has become relatively easy to find memorable traditional Asian cuisine, it's been a much harder task finding inspired Mexican fare, perhaps because of the city's proximity to Tijuana. Thus, the welcoming embrace given to Amigos Seafood and El Agave, who have both set up kitchens in Old Town and offer impressive regional interpretations.

Still, the cuisine of choice in this city is Italian and it has been so ever since we learned to say "pasta" without feeling self-conscious. As if proof is needed of *cucina Italiana's* dominance, look no further than Fifth Avenue – a virtual trattoria row, populated by longtime charmers such as Bella Luna and Osteria Panevino, who have been joined by fresher faces like de Medici – or, of course, Little Italy, where Cafe Zucchero, Trattoria Fantastica and Vicino Mare have opened their doors.

But a recent Gallic renaissance has gladdened the hearts of many an unreconstructed Francophile who was fearing that haute French fare was headed on its way out. In fact, posh El Bizcocho in Rancho Bernardo was rated the city's top restaurant for food this year, the chic WineSellar & Brasserie in Sorrento Mesa ranked second and the beautiful Mille Fleurs in Rancho Sante Fe tied for the third spot. Meanwhile, at the once-faded Le Fontainebleau at Downtown's swanky Westgate Hotel, Rene Herbeck has just taken over the range and already his magical marriage of modern and classic styles has joyously rejuvenated the venerable room. And savory solace at slightly less lofty prices can be found at newcomers like Jean-Michel Diot's breezy Tapenade in La Jolla and Fabrice Poigin's warm Vignola in the Gaslamp Quarter.

Speaking of prices, diners appear to appreciate the overall reasonableness of this city's restaurant tariffs. Compared with the average tab for a meal in other major Californian cities – in San Francisco, it costs $28.49 and in Los Angeles, $24.86 – it's affordable to eat out in SD, where that same meal costs $20.63. Further, among the 20 best values here, the average bill drops down to $10.22. And if you want to go really low-budget, amble down to Little Italy and order one of those Italian grinders on a hard roll. Nowadays, particularly if you let this *Survey* be your guide, you'll probably get exactly what you asked for. *Mangia*!

San Diego, CA   David Nelson
February 17, 1999

Key to Ratings/Symbols

This sample entry identifies the various types of
information contained in your Zagat Survey.

(1) Restaurant Name, Address & Phone Number

(2) Hours & Credit Cards

(3) ZAGAT Ratings

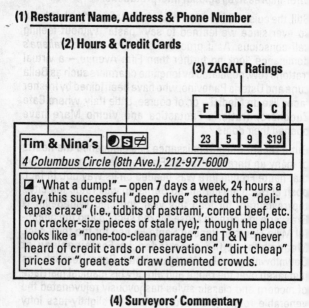

		F	D	S	C
		23	5	9	$19

Tim & Nina's ◑Ⓢⳛ

4 Columbus Circle (8th Ave.), 212-977-6000

■ "What a dump!" – open 7 days a week, 24 hours a
day, this successful "deep dive" started the "deli-
tapas craze" (i.e., tidbits of pastrami, corned beef, etc.
on cracker-size pieces of stale rye); though the place
looks like a "none-too-clean garage" and T & N "never
heard of credit cards or reservations", "dirt cheap"
prices for "great eats" draw demented crowds.

(4) Surveyors' Commentary

The names of restaurants with the highest overall ratings,
greatest popularity and importance are printed in **CAPITAL
LETTERS**. Address and phone numbers are printed in *italics*.

(2) Hours & Credit Cards

After each restaurant name you will find the following
courtesy information:

◑ .... *serving after 11 PM*

Ⓢ .... *open on Sunday*

Ⳛ .... *no credit cards accepted*

(3) ZAGAT Ratings

Food, Decor and **Service** are each rated on a scale of **0** to **30**:

F	D	S	C

F	.... *Food*
D	.... *Decor*
S	.... *Service*
C	.... *Cost*

23	5	9	$19

0 - 9	.... *poor to fair*
10 - 15	.... *fair to good*
16 - 19	.... *good to very good*
20 - 25	.... *very good to excellent*
26 - 30	.... *extraordinary to perfection*

▽ 23	5	9	$19

▽ .... *Low number of votes/less reliable*

The **Cost** (**C**) column reflects the estimated price of a dinner with one drink and tip. Lunch usually costs 25% less.

A restaurant listed without ratings is either an important **newcomer** or a popular **write-in**. The estimated cost, with one drink and tip, is indicated by the following symbols.

–	–	–	VE

I	.... *$15 and below*
M	.... *$16 to $30*
E	.... *$31 to $50*
VE	.... *$51 or more*

(4) Surveyors' Commentary

Surveyors' comments are summarized, with literal comments shown in quotation marks. The following symbols indicate whether responses were mixed or uniform.

◪ .... *mixed*
◼ .... *uniform*

San Diego's Most Popular

Bellefleur
Carlsbad

0　　Miles　　4

Rancho
Bernardo

Mille Fleurs
Delicias ★★
Rancho Santa Fe

El Bizcocho
Souplantation*

★
Rancho Valencia

Solana
Beach ★

Pamplemousse Grille
Fish Market

Jake's
Del Mar ★
★ Pacifica Del Mar
Del Mar

Brigantine*
Poway ★

George's at the Cove
La Valencia
Top o' the Cove
Trattoria Acqua

WineSellar &
Brasserie
★

CALIFORNIA

★★ P.F. Chang's
Cafe ┌ Tutto Mare
Japengo

★★
La ┘ Marine Room
Jolla Piatti

Pacific
Beach

Baci
★

Cafe ★ Kemo
Pacifica Sabe
★★
Belgian ★ ┌ California Cuisine
Lion ★ Montanas
Thee Mixx★★
Bungalow ★ Laurel

Point Loma

Coronado

San Diego

Pacific
Ocean

San
Diego
Bay

National
City

Anthony's
Star of
the Sea ★
Ruth's Chris

Ash St.

Fifth Ave.

Downtown
San Diego

★ Azzura Point

Rainwater's ★★
Broadway

Dobson's ★ Fio's
Sammy's Pizza
G St.

Market St.
Blue Point Coastal ★

Morton's
of Chicago ★

Top of
the Market

Harbor Dr.

Imperial
Beach

* Check for other locations

MEXICO

Most Popular Restaurants

Each of our reviewers has been asked to name his or her five favorite restaurants. The 40 spots most frequently named, in order of their popularity, are:

1. George's at the Cove
2. Mille Fleurs
3. Laurel
4. Pamplemousse Grille
5. WineSellar/Brasserie
6. Cafe Japengo
7. Trattoria Acqua
8. Belgian Lion
9. El Bizcocho
10. Rainwater's
11. Azzura Point
12. Marine Room
13. Rancho Valencia
14. Piatti
15. Dobson's
16. Pacifica Del Mar
17. Fish Market
18. California Cuisine
19. Delicias*
20. Kemo Sabe

21. Mixx*
22. Blue Point Coastal
23. Tutto Mare*
24. Top o' the Cove
25. Ruth's Chris
26. Thee Bungalow*
27. Cafe Pacifica
28. Anthony's Star of the Sea
29. P.F. Chang's*
30. Brigantine
31. Morton's of Chicago*
32. Montanas
33. Jake's Del Mar
34. Baci
35. La Valencia*
36. Top of the Market
37. Fio's
38. Souplantation
39. Bellefleur
40. Sammy's Pizza

It's obvious that many of the restaurants on the above list are among the most expensive, but San Diego diners also love a bargain. Were popularity calibrated to price, we suspect that a number of other restaurants would join the above ranks. Thus, we have listed over 105 Best Buys on pages 17–18.

* Tied with the restaurant listed directly above it.

Top Ratings*

Top 40 Food Ranking

28	El Bizcocho		Dobson's
27	WineSellar/Brasserie		Cafe Pacifica
	Mille Fleurs		Top of the Market
	Sushi Ota**		Old Trieste
	Azzura Point	24	Pacifica Del Mar
	Pamplemousse Grille		Top o' the Cove
26	Rancho Valencia		Baily Wine Country Cafe
	George's at the Cove		California Cuisine
	Belgian Lion		Trattoria Acqua
	Bread & Cie.		Baci
	Laurel		Emerald Chinese**
	Taka		La Bonne Bouffe**
	Morton's of Chicago		French Market Grille
25	Come On In!		Bernard'O
	Salvatore's		Sushi on the Rock
	Cafe Japengo		Point Loma Seafoods
	Thee Bungalow		150 Grand Café
	Rainwater's		Maitre D'
	Delicias		La Fonda
	Ruth's Chris	23	Spice & Rice

Top Spots by Cuisine

American (New)
26 George's at the Cove
25 Dobson's
24 150 Grand Café
23 La Valencia
22 Cafe Champagne

American (Regional)
27 Pamplemousse Grille
24 Pacifica Del Mar
   Baily Wine Country Cafe
23 Dining Room
   Pacific Coast Grill

American (Traditional)
23 Kono's Cafe
   Red Tracton's
22 Lael's
20 Bully's
   Mission Hills Café

BBQ
18 Claim Jumper
17 Tony Roma's
16 Hang Ten
   Kansas City BBQ
13 Eric's Ribs

Breakfast†
25 Come On In!
23 Kono's Cafe
22 Mission
21 Cafe Zinc
19 Hob Nob Hill

Brunch
28 El Bizcocho
26 Rancho Valencia
25 Top of the Market
24 Pacifica Del Mar
   Top o' the Cove

---

* Excluding restaurants with low voting.
** Tied with the restaurant listed directly above it.
† Other than hotels.

12

Californian

27 Azzura Point
　　Pamplemousse Grille
26 Rancho Valencia
25 Come On In!
　　Delicias

Chinese

24 Emerald Chinese
23 Jasmine
22 Panda Inn
21 Panda Country
　　P.F. Chang's

Coffee Shops/Diners

21 Big Kitchen
19 Crest Cafe
　　Hob Nob Hill
18 Living Room
17 Ruby's Diner

Continental

26 Rancho Valencia
24 Top o' the Cove
21 Chez Loma
　　Crown Room
20 Mister A's

Delis/Sandwich Shops

22 D.Z. Akin's
16 Canora's
　　Milton's Deli
　　City Delicatessen
15 Samson's

Eclectic/International

26 Taka
23 Mixx
22 Mission
　　Parkhouse Eatery
19 Torrey Pines Cafe

Family Dining

23 Kono's Cafe
22 Sammy's Pizza
19 Souplantation
18 California Pizza Kit.
17 Corvette Diner

French

28 El Bizcocho
26 Belgian Lion
25 Thee Bungalow
24 La Bonne Bouffe
　　Maitre D'

French Bistros/Cafes

26 Bread & Cie.
24 French Market Grille
21 French Gourmet
19 La Vache & Co.
18 La Provence

French (New)

28 El Bizcocho
27 WineSellar/Brasserie
　　Mille Fleurs
　　Pamplemousse Grille
26 Laurel

Hamburgers

21 Hodad's
20 Bully's
18 Hamburger Mary's
17 Johnny Rockets
　　Corvette Diner

Hotel Dining

28 El Bizcocho
　　Rancho Bernardo Inn
27 Azzura Point
　　Loews Coronado Bay
26 Rancho Valencia
　　Rancho Valencia
23 Dining Room
　　L'Auberge Del Mar
　　Grant Grill
　　U.S. Grant Hotel

Indian

22 Bombay
21 KC's Tandoor
19 Star of India
15 Ashoka Cuisine of India
– Maharajah

Italian

25 Salvatore's
　　Old Trieste
24 Trattoria Acqua
　　Baci
23 Bell'agio

Japanese

27 Sushi Ota
26 Taka
25 Cafe Japengo
24 Sushi on the Rock
22 Mr. Sushi

13

Top Food

Mexican/Tex-Mex
24 La Fonda
22 El Agave
20 Miguel's Cocina
     Chilango's
     El Indio Shop

Newcomers/Rated
27 Pamplemousse Grille
26 Morton's of Chicago
24 French Market Grille
     La Fonda
23 Mixx

Newcomers/Unrated
     Gulf Coast Grill
     Jin Sang
     Palomino Euro Bistro
     Roppongi
     Tapenade

People-Watching
27 Mille Fleurs
     Pamplemousse Grille
26 George's at the Cove
25 Cafe Japengo
     Dobson's

Pizza
23 Cafe Zucchero
22 Vigilucci's Pizzeria
     Sammy's Pizza
20 Carino's
     Embers Grille

Power Lunch
25 Rainwater's
     Dobson's
23 Grant Grill
22 Le Fontainebleau
20 St. James Bar/Rest.

Seafood
25 Cafe Pacifica
     Top of the Market
24 Pacifica Del Mar
     Point Loma Seafoods
23 Anthony's Star of the Sea

Southwestern
22 Kemo Sabe
21 Cilantros
     Dakota
     Epazote
18 Coyote B&G

Steakhouses
26 Morton's of Chicago
25 Rainwater's
     Ruth's Chris
23 Red Tracton's
20 Bully's

Thai
23 Spice & Rice
     Spices Thai Cafe
     Saffron Chicken
22 Thai House Cuisine
21 Karinya

Worth a Drive
28 El Bizcocho
     Rancho Bernardo
27 Mille Fleurs
     Rancho Santa Fe
     Azzura Point
     Coronado
26 Rancho Valencia
     Rancho Santa Fe
25 Delicias
     Rancho Santa Fe

Top 40 Decor Ranking

29	Rancho Valencia	
27	Field	
	Mille Fleurs	
26	Marine Room	
	El Bizcocho	
	Delicias	
	Azzura Point	
	George's at the Cove	
	Le Fontainebleau	
	Laurel	
	Top o' the Cove	
25	Crown Room	
	Vivace	
	Peohe's	
	La Valencia	
	California Bistro	
24	Cafe Japengo	
	Grant Grill	
	Trattoria Acqua	
	Top of the Market	

	Morton's of Chicago
	Pacifica Del Mar
	Prince of Wales Grill
	Pamplemousse Grille
23	Salvatore's
	Il Fornaio
	Karl Strauss Brew. Gardens
	Dining Room
	Blue Point Coastal
	Corvette Diner
	Shores, The
	Jake's Del Mar
	Mister A's
	Kemo Sabe
	Piatti
	Crescent Shores Grill
	Maitre D'
	Sally's*
22	Tutto Mare
	Casa De Bandini

Outdoor

Cafe Champagne	Il Fornaio
California Cuisine	La Valencia
Chez Loma	Pacifica del Mar
Delicias	Rancho Valencia
Epazote	Sante
George's at the Cove	Top of the Market
Green Flash	Trattoria Acqua

Romantic

Anthony's Star of the Sea	Maitre D'
Baci	Mille Fleurs
Delicias	Prince of Wales Grill
El Bizcocho	Rancho Valencia
Grant Grill	Sante
La Valencia, Sky Room	Top o' the Cove
Le Fontainebleau	Vivace

Rooms

Azzura Point	Le Fontainebleau
Delicias	Mille Fleurs
El Bizcocho	Mister A's
Grant Grill	Prince of Wales Grill
Humphrey's	Rainwater's
Laurel	Sante
La Valencia, Sky Room	Trattoria Acqua

---

* Tied with the restaurant listed directly above it.

Top Decor

Views

Beach House
Brockton Villa
Charlie's by the Sea
Chart House
Crab Catcher
Epazote
George's at the Cove

Jake's Del Mar
La Valencia, Sky Room
Mister A's
Pacifica del Mar
Peohe's
Rusty Pelican
Top o' the Cove

Top 40 Service Ranking

26 El Bizcocho
Mille Fleurs
25 Rancho Valencia
Azzura Point
Pamplemousse Grille
WineSellar/Brasserie
George's at the Cove
Morton's of Chicago
24 Delicias
Rainwater's
Maitre D'
Le Fontainebleau
23 Belgian Lion
Baci
Anthony's Star of the Sea
Old Trieste
Dining Room
La Valencia
Sante
Thee Bungalow

Salvatore's
150 Grand Café
Top o' the Cove
Grant Grill
California Cuisine
Dobson's
Top of the Market
Prince of Wales Grill
Primavera
22 Cafe Pacifica
Laurel
Mister A's
California Bistro
Marine Room
Firenze
Kono's Cafe
Piatti
Chez Loma
Thai House
Fifth & Hawthorn

80 Top Bangs For The Buck

This list reflects the best dining values in our *Survey*. It is produced by dividing the cost of a meal into the combined ratings for food, decor and service.

1. Kono's Cafe
2. Bread & Cie.
3. Hodad's
4. Come On In!
5. Karen Krasne's
6. Living Room
7. Rubio's Baja Grill
8. Big Kitchen
9. Mission Hills Café
10. Fins
11. San Diego Chicken Pie
12. Cafe 222
13. La Salsa
14. El Indio
15. Daily's
16. Chuey's
17. Souplantation
18. Johnny Rockets
19. Ruby's
20. Cafe Zinc
21. Noodle Hse./Otemoyan
22. Field
23. Point Loma Seafoods
24. Saffron Chicken
25. Ichiban
26. Pasta Pronto
27. Cottage
28. Anthony's Fishette
29. John's Waffle Shop
30. Spice & Rice
31. KC's Tandoor
32. Corvette Diner
33. Oscar's
34. Las Olas
35. Crest Cafe
36. Cafe Zucchero
37. Soup Exchange
38. Filippi's
39. Lotsa Pasta
40. Thai House
41. Old Spaghetti Factory
42. China Inn
43. Fairouz Cafe
44. Downtown Johnny Brown's
45. St. Germain's Cafe
46. Callahan's Pub
47. Hamburger Mary's
48. Jimmy Carter's
49. Islands Fine Burgers
50. Rancho El Nopal
51. Canora's Sandwich Shop
52. Carino's
53. D.Z. Akin's
54. Ingrid's
55. Little Tokyo
56. City Deli
57. Hob Nob Hill
58. Casa de Pico
59. Peking Palace
60. Adam's Steak & Eggs
61. Pizzeria Uno
62. Rimel's Rotisserie
63. Chilango's
64. Old Town Mexican Cafe
65. Miguel's Cocina
66. Panda Country
67. Karl Strauss' Brew. & Grill
68. Jose's Courtroom
69. Andre's Cuban
70. Taco Auctioneer
71. Pizza Nova
72. Sammy's Pizza
73. Tony's Jacal
74. Brockton Villa
75. Crocodile Cafe
76. Spices Thai Cafe
77. Phuong Trang
78. Bombay
79. California Pizza Kit.
80. Khyber Pass Afghan

Additional Good Values

(A bit more expensive, but worth every penny)

A-Dong

Aesop's Tables

Bistro Yang

Cafe on Park

Casa De Bandini

China Camp at Fat City

Coyote Bar & Grill

D'Lish Bistro

Elephant Bar

El Fandango

El Tecolote

Embers Grille

Fidel's

Firehouse Beach Cafe

Hang Ten

HomeTown Buffet

Karl Strauss' Brew. Gardens

La Jolla Brewing Co.

Lorna's Italian Kitchen

Panda Inn

Royal Thai

San Diego Brewing Co.

Taste of Thai

Trophy's

Vegetarian Zone

Venetian Restaurant

Yakitori II

Zagarella

Alphabetical
Directory of
Restaurants

Adam's Avenue Grill S
— | — | — | M

(fka Grill 2201)
2201 Adams Ave. (Mississippi St.), 619-298-8440
A change in proprietors netted the former Grill 2201 a new name, along with a reputation to uphold as a "good neighborhood place"; boasting a "creative" New American menu and service that's "getting a little better", it keeps casual regulars from surrounding Normal Heights faithful with "good value", a lively mood and "great desserts."

Adam's Steak & Eggs S M
16 | 8 | 18 | $12

Travelodge, 1201 Hotel Circle S. (I-8), 619-291-1103
☑ "All-American breakfasts" are the one and only attraction at this "crowded", sparsely appointed Mission Valley monument to cholesterol-era cuisine, where "long waits" followed by "good, quick" service are the norm; it's especially popular for "family Sunday" interludes, but some caution that this "tourist trap" is "nothing special."

A-Dong S
20 | 7 | 15 | $12

3874 Fairmount Ave. (University Ave.), 619-298-4420
☑ "The food, not the ambiance" is the charm at this City Heights Vietnamese, which wins kudos for "authentic" eats from a "huge menu" ("takes an hour to read") that offers some exotic choices; a few, though, find the location in a "scary" section of town a bit "less appetizing."

Aesop's Tables Greek Cafe S M
20 | 16 | 18 | $17

Costa Verde Shopping Ctr., 8650 Genesee Ave. (La Jolla Village Dr.), Golden Triangle, 619-455-1535
☑ "Opa!" is the rallying cry for a "Greek treat" at this "informal" entry in the busy Golden Triangle; the merguez sausage and *saganaki* (flaming cheese) are "great stuff", and the "pleasant surroundings" and "good service" lend a "feel-at-home" air to the crowded dining areas; however, a few detractors declare that "Zorba would be upset" at the staff's "get 'em in, get 'em out" approach.

Aladdin Mediterranean Cafe S M
19 | 13 | 16 | $16

5420 Clairemont Mesa Blvd. (1 block west of I-805), 619-573-0000
☑ "An oasis in taco land", this "authentic Middle Eastern" Clairemonter is regarded as "unique in the area" and "good" for hummus and tabbouleh; crowded and "noisy", it's a "place for lunch or takeout", and if the "decor leaves something to be desired", "large portions" compensate.

Albie's Beef Inn M
18 | 11 | 20 | $19

Travelodge, 1201 Hotel Circle S. (I-8), 619-291-1103
☑ A "throwback to a bygone era", this "unpretentious" Mission Valley chophouse functions as a "meeting place" for aficionados of "traditional meat and potatoes"; the "value isn't bad" and the old-pro servers get the job done efficiently, but the "tourists in Bermudas" and "nudes on the walls" make for unusual dining companions.

Alfonso's 🅂🅼   17 | 13 | 17 | $17
1251 Prospect St. (bet. Cave St. & Ivanhoe Ave.), La Jolla, 619-454-2232
☑ The jammed sidewalk terrace at this "friendly, peppy" "La Jolla institution" offers "great people-watching", as well as some of the "best margaritas" around and a *carne asada* burrito "to die for"; though nonfans dub it "perfect – for out-of-towners", the cheerful service moves loyalists to declare the place "a weekly must" for a Mexican experience.

Amigos Seafood 🅂🅼   – | – | – | I
2470 San Diego Ave. (Conde St.), 619-260-3624
As a purveyor of Baja California–style finfish and shellfish, this "awesome new spot in Old Town" stands alone with "savory", "inspired" fare, such as *siete mares* ('seven seas', a lush seafood soup), "superb shrimp *de ajo*" (sauteed in garlic butter) and, for those who like "lots of spice", shrimp dressed with hot serrano chili sauce; though the "margaritas are wonderful" and the room pleasantly colorful, the green service needs improvement.

Andiamo!! 🅂   ▽ 22 | 16 | 16 | $18
Tierra del Sol Mall, 10425 Tierrasanta Blvd. (Santo Rd.), 619-277-3501
■ Boosters of this "little oasis in Tierrasanta" call it "a real gem" that's valued for its "gourmet-style Italian" fare; graced with "subtle spices", the classic Tuscan cooking outshines the sometimes "amateurish" service, but otherwise this is a comfy choice for suburban dining within striking distance of Qualcomm Stadium.

Andre's Cuban Restaurant 🅂🅼   18 | 9 | 18 | $13
1235 Morena Blvd. (Dorcas St.), 619-275-4114
☑ Priced right but decor-free, this "pleasant, friendly" Cuban in the commercial Morena district serves standards like black beans and rice; connoisseurs concede it's "not Miami", but this is the "closest to Cuba that SD has" – not least because it's the "only game in town."

Anthony's Fishette 🅂🅼   16 | 14 | 14 | $10
1360 N. Harbor Dr. (Ash St.), 619-232-5103
☑ Its location on the Downtown waterfront may be "the best thing about" this docksider, though the "cheap fish 'n' chips" and other "quick seafood meals" explain why it runs full speed ahead; the "fresh air" out on the sunny patio is agreeable, except when aggressive seagulls "try to share your meal."

Anthony's Fish Grotto 🅂🅼   17 | 15 | 17 | $18
11666 Avena Pl. (Bernardo Ctr. Dr.), 619-451-2070
1360 N. Harbor Dr. (Ash St.), 619-232-5103
(Continues)

Anthony's Fish Grotto (Cont.)
215 W. Bay Blvd. (E St. & Hwy. 5), Chula Vista, 619-425-4200
9530 Murray Dr. (Hwy. 8 & Severin Dr.), La Mesa, 619-463-0368
◪ "Unbeatable value for plain, fresh seafood" sums up the
popular appeal of this long-running area chain, which rates
high with the "early-bird and senior discount crowd" and
amounts to a "tourist Mecca" for visitors on a "modest
budget"; some branches could stand to "redo the decor",
but the "quick service" and "no-surprises" approach make
them a "safe" pick for family expeditions.

ANTHONY'S STAR   23 | 22 | 23 | $39
OF THE SEA 🅂🅼
1360 N. Harbor Dr. (Ash St.), 619-232-7408
◪ A "classic" place to "impress out-of-towners" on the
Downtown waterfront, this "pricey", 30-year-old seafooder
has a "formal" mood and jacket-suggested policy that help
retain the favor of a well-heeled crowd; while some miss
"the old menu", others find the food "improved" since the
arrival of a Ritz-Carlton chef, and a redo set for early '99
should please those who dismiss the "'60s" decor.

Arrivederci 🅂🅼   22 | 17 | 20 | $21
3845 Fourth Ave. (University Ave.), 619-299-6282
■ This "little spot" in trendy Hillcrest is "consistently solid",
serving "Italian food like mama makes" in a "quaint setting"
where the staff makes the most of its "charming accents";
it's an "authentic" experience and a "good value", so wave
ciao to your neighbors – the "tables are very close."

Ashoka Cuisine of India 🅂   15 | 13 | 15 | $17
8008 Girard Ave. (Prospect St.), La Jolla, 619-454-6263
◪ There is little agreement as to whether this Indian with a
fine view of La Jolla Cove offers an "authentic" taste of the
Raj or "barely passable" fare; however, there is a consensus
that it's moderately priced and plainly decorated.

Ashoka the Great 🅂🅼   ▽ 20 | 15 | 16 | $15
9474 Black Mountain Rd. (Miramar Rd.), 619-695-9749
■ Loyalists like this "reliable" Mira Mesa Indian's "large
menu" of "good, spicy and tasty" cuisine ("excellent
breads") and say it's an affordable choice for "quick,
casual" dining "with the kids"; although it feels like a
neighborhood spot, it packs in patrons from all around,
so be patient.

Asmara 🅂🅼⇗   – | – | – | I
4433 El Cajon Blvd. (bet. Fairmount & Highland Aves.),
619-563-3666
Given San Diego's shortage of similar options, this budget-
friendly City Heights entry offers an "outstanding Ethiopian
experience", at least on local terms; the crowd ranges from
laid-back types to livelier regulars who come to "get
rowdy" in the casual environment.

Asti Ristorante ◐ [S] [M] 17 | 15 | 16 | $27
728 Fifth Ave. (bet. F & G Sts.), 619-232-8844
◪ Located on the hottest block in the oh-so-sizzling Gaslamp Quarter, this Italian features "good seafood" and "great wines", but risks being labeled "one of too many look-alikes" in a trattoria-heavy neighborhood; the sidewalk patio is fine for taking in the "interesting street scene", but indoor diners are confronted with crowded conditions.

Athens Market Taverna [S] [M] 20 | 16 | 19 | $20
109 W. F St. (bet. 1st Ave. & Front St.), 619-234-1955
◪ Proprietor Mary Pappas has made this Downtowner "everybody's favorite Greek hangout" with her "authentic" cooking and generous portions ("my thighs may explode"); while "friendly service" keeps the "fun" atmosphere alive, a few naysayers gripe that it's "past its prime."

AZZURA POINT [S] 27 | 26 | 25 | $45
Loews Coronado Bay Resort, 4000 Coronado Bay Rd. (Silver Strand Blvd.), Coronado, 619-424-4477
■ This airy room on the second floor of the view-endowed Loews Coronado Bay Resort is where "serious" foodies join hotel guests for chef James Boyce's "innovative" Cal-Med fare as well as some "great sunsets"; it's a "special-occasion vacation in our hometown" that's even more appealing now with the "smashing new decor."

BACI RISTORANTE [M] 24 | 20 | 23 | $31
1955 W. Morena Blvd. (Ashton St.), 619-275-2094
■ "Romantic and cozy" Italian that's a "hidden gem" where "rich, full-flavored" cooking, "impeccable service" and "old-fashioned elegance" reign; despite its less than convenient Morena locale ("halfway between La Jolla and Mission Valley"), it remains a "longtime favorite."

BAILY WINE COUNTRY CAFE [S] [M] 24 | 18 | 21 | $22
Temecula Town Ctr., 27644 Ynez Rd. (Rancho California Rd.), Temecula, 909-676-9567
■ "In an area with only chain restaurants", this "wonderful oasis" in a Temecula shopping center offers "top-notch" "California-style" cuisine that seemingly "gets better every year"; the setting is "intimate" and the staff is "excellent", plus at these prices, the "casual" wine country clientele can afford to sample the "great" selection of local vintages.

Bai Yook [S] [M] ▽ 22 | 14 | 17 | $11
1260 University Ave. (bet. Richmond & Vermont Sts.), 619-296-2700
◪ Noted for its "great presentation" of tasty Thai cooking, this purse-pleasing newcomer on a lively Hillcrest block draws an eclectic crowd that appreciates the "excellent value"; however, the "small but pretty" room can get cramped on busy nights.

Bali Authentic Indonesian Cuisine [S][M] 18 | 18 | 19 | $24

Village Corner, 7660 Fay Ave. (Kline St.), La Jolla, 619-454-4540

■ Offering the "only Indonesian food in town", this "interesting" spot on a La Jolla side street serves up "delicious" rijsttafel as the house specialty; the "warm welcome" proffered by the staff is just as appealing as the "attractive" decor showcasing Balinese artwork.

Bandar ☾ [S][M] 20 | 18 | 17 | $20

825 Fourth Ave. (bet. E & F Sts.), 619-238-0101

■ A "wonderful addition to the Gaslamp Quarter" that provides an "elegant introduction to Persian dining", this "quiet, relaxing" and "consistently good" restaurant is crowded at noontime thanks to the "great lunch deals" and "gracious" service; the decor aims for "understated sophistication" (for that matter, so does the clientele).

Bangkok Thai Cuisine [S][M] ▽ 17 | 14 | 18 | $13

4656 Mission Blvd. (bet. Diamond & Emerald Sts.), Pacific Beach, 619-581-1401

◪ Known for its "dependable Thai" cooking, this casual, easy-on-the-budget Pacific Beacher wins respect for its readiness to "make it hot when you ask"; the "restful decor" seems to agree with the tanned, young patrons, though the well-traveled sniff it's "not like Thailand."

Banzai Cantina [S][M] 16 | 13 | 15 | $18

3667 India St. (bet I-5 & Washington St.), 619-298-6388

◪ "Funky fun" awaits at the upper end of India Street in the form of a "weird but good" hodgepodge of Japanese and Mexican; the "unique menu items" are "quick and tasty", though the cooking sometimes "falls short of expectations" ("is it banzai or hari kari?"); come sundown, though, the "great happy hour" and "cheap" prices are all that this crowd needs to know.

Bayou Bar & Grill [S][M] 21 | 17 | 19 | $22

329 Market St. (bet. 3rd & 4th Sts.), 619-696-8747

■ This Gaslamp Quarter Cajun-Creole will "take you back to New Orleans even if you've never been there"; besides the "pleasant change from bland foods", "visitors love" the Big Easy memorabilia covering the walls, the recorded jazz and the "intimate yet fun" atmosphere – when you're in a Mardi Gras mood, it's "tops."

Beach House, The [S][M] 16 | 21 | 17 | $22

2530 S. Coast Hwy. 101 (bet. Chesterfield & Lomas Santa Fe Drs.), Cardiff-by-the-Sea, 760-753-1321

◪ An "amazing view of the ocean" sets the scene at this beachfront American in Cardiff, and the "fantastic surfside tables" seem to account for most of its popularity; no wonder the merely "adequate" SoCal fare can't compete with "romantic evenings" "at high tide."

BELGIAN LION, THE 26 | 21 | 23 | $36

2265 Bacon St. (W. Point Loma Blvd.), 619-223-2700

◪ "Expensive but very good" Belgian-French in Ocean Beach that reminds some of "grandma's parlor" with its lace doily–strewn setting, but most ignore the setting and enjoy "wonderful cassoulet" and other "hearty" fare; though some claim service isn't always doting, fans revel in "personal attention" and find this Coulon family veteran "still great"; open Thursday–Saturday, dinner only.

Bell'agio [S][M] 23 | 16 | 19 | $21

10492 Clairemont Mesa Blvd. (Santo Rd.), 619-268-8984

■ "Don't let the strip mall location fool you" – this "friendly, dependable" Italian aims to please with "upscale" food that's "authentic and consistently good"; the oft-noted "great bread" and "pleasant" environment make it a "home away from home" for committed loyalists.

Bella Luna [S][M] 22 | 20 | 20 | $26

748 Fifth Ave. (bet. F & G Sts.), 619-239-3222

■ Located in the Gaslamp Quarter's "pasta ghetto", this "favorite" "stands out among the plethora" of neighboring clones for its "excellent" "regional Italian cooking"; it can be "cozy despite the Fifth Avenue crowds" surging past the sidewalk tables, but a "noisy, frantic atmosphere" may ensue when conventioneers descend.

Bellefleur Winery & Restaurant [S][M] 21 | 21 | 18 | $27

Carlsbad Co. Stores, 5610 Paseo del Norte (bet. Cannon & Palomar Airport Rds.), Carlsbad, 760-603-1919

◪ An "interesting newcomer", this Tuscan villa–like Carlsbad "destination" earns praise for its "big portions of wine country cuisine"; the "great food and ambiance" offer relief "after a full day of shopping", but "bring your earplugs" in case it gets "loud."

Benihana of Tokyo [S][M] 19 | 19 | 20 | $25

477 Caminio del Rio S. (Mission Ctr. Rd.), 619-298-4666

◪ "Great fun for birthday parties and big groups" enthuse those who applaud the "good show" and the teppanyaki at this "kitschy" Mission Valley Japanese; dissenters say the "theatrical" effects distract from chow that's "very ordinary" and "not really Japanese", while the "corny patter" may be best for "friends from out of town."

Bennigan's ◐ [S][M] 12 | 14 | 14 | $14

1760 Camino del Rio N. (bet. Mission Ctr. Dr. & Texas St.), 619-291-8853

◪ "Standard chain food" is about all that most surveyors expect of this "noisy" American "meet market" in Mission Valley; a hub "for hanging out" "if you're 22", especially during the popular happy hour, it's called "inexpensive and friendly" by those who come in "for a quick bite" and run down the menu's long list of "good apps."

Bernard'O Restaurant
24 | 20 | 21 | $27

12457 Rancho Bernardo Rd. (Pomerado Rd.), Rancho Bernardo, 619-487-7171

■ Temporarily closed and sorely missed by a clientele that "can't wait until it's back" (slated for February 1999, after the renovated Rancho Bernardo shopping center that houses it reopens), this Contemporary Gallic has a reputation for "always providing an enjoyable experience" with "excellent food for the price"; devotees pray the new incarnation will remain inland North County's own "lovely Country French gem."

Berta's S
21 | 13 | 17 | $18

3928 Twiggs St. (Congress St.), 619-295-2343

■ "Don't come lookin' for tacos" at this "unique" Old Town eatery, which "gets points for being different" thanks to a far "from ordinary" menu that offers a "little of everything Latin American" (e.g. Chilean *pastel de choclo,* Brazilian *vatapá*); adventurous types are "delighted and surprised" at the "pleasant" experience; P.S. the minuscule "patio beats the inside" dining area.

Big Kitchen S M⊄
21 | 17 | 21 | $11

3003 Grape St. (bet. Fern & 30th Sts.), 619-234-5789

■ A "great hole-in-the-wall" where a pre-stardom Whoopi Goldberg washed dishes and proprietor "Judy the Beauty" "makes everyone feel like a regular", this Eclectic breakfast-and-luncher in Golden Hill is celebrated as "the closest thing to Berkeley anywhere in Southern California" by its hip, urban clientele; "you won't go away hungry" thanks to the "homestyle cooking", and while there may be "waits on weekends", the "funny, sassy waitresses" do their best to make it up to you.

Bird Rock Cafe S M
20 | 16 | 19 | $23

5656 La Jolla Blvd. (Bird Rock Ave.), La Jolla, 619-551-4090

▣ This "charming neighborhood restaurant" in the Bird Rock district of La Jolla attracts well-clad but casual locals with a menu of Eclectic "Americana" that's best when hands-on chef-owner Chuck Samuelson is manning the stove ; while critics counter that it's "not as good as it used to be", it's "affordable" and the option of ordering most items in medium or full portions is a crowd-pleaser.

Bistro Yang S M
20 | 18 | 17 | $17

Clairemont Town Sq., 4705-G Clairemont Dr. (Clairemont Mesa Blvd.), 619-483-6893

▣ Supporters call the "California-style Chinese" cooking at this East-West fusion "innovative" and "tasty", and the "upscale, trendy" ambiance makes it a "surprising" addition to busy Clairemont; the crowd on its way to or from the neighboring multiplex has no problem with a "yuppified" setting and knows owner "Charlie [Yang] wants to please."

B.J.'s Pizza & Grill S M 15 | 13 | 14 | $14
La Jolla Village Ctr., 8873 Villa La Jolla Dr. (bet. La Jolla Village & Nobel Drs.), La Jolla, 619-455-0662

◪ Loyalists like the specialty "pizzookie for dessert" served up at this "casual" UC student hangout in La Jolla, but foes feel that the deep-dish pies are only "passable"; all agree that fare geared to "keep you going before or after the movies" ensures that this "fun", "friendly place" is "always full of people", despite service that can be "a little slow."

Blue Bird Cafe S M ▽ 18 | 14 | 17 | $15
646 Valley Ave. (bet. Genevieve & Vera Sts.), Solana Beach, 619-755-4426

◪ The menu "hasn't changed" in decades at this Mexican "dump" in the Eden Gardens neighborhood of Solana Beach, which suits its longtime aficionados who chirp about "above-average", "authentic fare" at "bargain" prices; however, those wary of the "empty" room (there never seems to be a "crowd") say the food is "just so-so."

Blue Crab S M 14 | 17 | 16 | $20
4922 N. Harbor Dr. (Nimitz Blvd.), 619-224-3000

◪ Set on the waterfront near Shelter Island, this casual seafood house affords a "beautiful view"; but while some like the "good luncheon and early-bird specials", most sigh that it's "a shame to waste this location" on such "ordinary dishes, tacky decor" and "extremely indifferent servers."

BLUE POINT 23 | 23 | 21 | $34
COASTAL CUISINE S M
565 Fifth Ave. (Market St.), 619-233-6623

◪ Despite high ratings, this "see-and-be-seen" seafood supper club draws very vocal differences of opinion: admirers say it's "a breath of fresh salt air for the Gaslamp Quarter", with "some of SD's best seafood", "fabulous martinis", a "posh" room and "understated class"; but critics counter that it's an "overrated and overpriced yuppie paradise" with maddeningly "uneven" food, "rude service" and excessive "noise.

Boathouse, The S M 18 | 19 | 17 | $23
2040 Harbor Island Dr. (Harbor Dr.), 619-291-8011

◪ Diners at this spacious, "pleasant" seafooder with a "great location" on Harbor Island are treated to "beautiful views" of the marina while ordering from a "reliable", "good-value" menu; however, critics carp that the fish is "nothing special" and "overpriced."

Bollicine Restaurant & Bar S M ▽ 16 | 14 | 11 | $20
8008 Girard Ave. (Prospect St.), La Jolla, 619-454-2222

◪ The "bubbles, bubbles everywhere" decor and the "patio with an ocean view" seem to be more "mesmerizing" than the "traditional" fare proffered at this casual, midpriced Northern Italian in La Jolla.

Bombay Exotic Cuisine of India S M | 22 | 19 | 19 | $18

Village Hillcrest Shopping Ctr., 3975 Fifth Ave. (University Ave.), 619-298-3155

■ Voted the "best Indian in SD", this "standout" in Hillcrest distinguishes itself with "zesty flavors", a "varied menu [try the tandoori fish and the "great breads"] with lots of vegetarian options" and a terrific lunch buffet "deal"; its followers insist that there's "nothing like it" in town, but some cynics say the "standard" dishes are "Americanized."

BREAD & CIE. S M⇩ | 26 | 14 | 17 | $9

350 University Ave. (4th Ave.), 619-683-9322

■ Because its "breads can't be beat", this "treasure" of a French bakery/cafe in Hillcrest is "worth a drive from anywhere" for the "myriad" variety of "first-class", "artisanal" loaves "with crunchy crusts" that are so irresistible, some "go early, inhale and smile"; "eat-in accommodations are minimal" and there's "no decor", so insiders advise: get the yeasty wonders to go and for "a cheap, filling lunch", pick up some "creative sandwiches."

Brigantine, The S M | 17 | 17 | 18 | $22

13445 Poway Rd. (Community Rd.), 619-486-3066
2444 San Diego Ave. (Conde St.), 619-298-9840
2725 Shelter Island Dr. (bet. Rosecrans Blvd. & Scott St.), 619-224-2871
1333 Orange Ave. (Adella Ave.), Coronado, 619-435-4166
3263 Camino Del Mar (Via de la Valle), Del Mar, 619-481-1166
421 W. Felicita Ave. (Centre City Pkwy.), Escondido, 760-743-4718
9350 Fuerte Dr. (Severin Dr.), La Mesa, 619-465-1935

◪ "Consistent and pleasant", this "lively", "reasonably priced" seafood chain features the "best fish tacos in the county", an "excellent happy hour" with "great bar food" and a "helpful" staff; however, critics complain about "assembly-line", "generic" fare and "hit-or-miss service."

Brockton Villa Restaurant S M | 19 | 21 | 17 | $17

1235 Coast Blvd. (Prospect Pl.), La Jolla, 619-454-7393

◪ "Don't leave La Jolla without watching a sunset" "from the terrace" of this "distinctive" 1894 beach cottage "hideaway" with "the prettiest coastal view" in town; "homey and comfortable", it turns out "super breakfasts" and "fantastic brunches ("eggs steamed on the espresso machine – wow!")", though reviewers say the "ho-hum" New American dishes on the lunch and dinner menus "don't live up to" the "beautiful ocean setting."

Bronx Pizza S M⇩ | – | – | – | I

111 Washington St. (bet. 1st & 3rd Aves.), 619-291-3341

"Fabulous, New York–style, crispy"-crusted pizza – perhaps the "best in San Diego" – is the claim to fame of this "inexpensive", little Hillcrest "hole-in-the-wall"; don't expect much in the way of atmosphere or even many seats (only 16), but for pies this good, who cares?

Budapest Express S   ▽ 10 | 11 | 12 | $18
315 S. Coast Hwy. 101 (Loma Santa Fe Dr.), Solana Beach, 619-259-4465

☑ Perhaps "nobody tries harder" than the staff at this "mom-and-pop" Solana Beach Hungarian that's housed in several "cute dining cars"; but while some delight in its "old-world charm and atmosphere" and find the "good-value" "home-cooked food" "tasty", many others say the "mediocre" fare is "greasy."

Buffalo Joe's S M   11 | 12 | 13 | $17
600 Fifth Ave. (Market St.), 619-236-1616

☑ "Better as a bar than a restaurant", this "loud" Gaslamp Quarter American is "perfect if you're in the mood for 10-cent wings" at happy hour; regulars advise "come for the music [performed live nightly], not the food" (the "BBQ is only fair"); though it can be a "fun place", be forewarned that the "brash" staff "sometimes doesn't have a clue."

Bully's ● S M   20 | 13 | 18 | $21
2401 Camino del Rio S. (Texas St.), 619-291-2665
1404 Camino del Mar (15th St.), Del Mar, 619-755-1660
5755 La Jolla Blvd. (Bird Rock Ave.), La Jolla, 619-459-2768

■ Refrains of the "best prime rib", "wonderful roast beef", "good steaks" and "can't-be-beat hamburgers" meld into a carnivorous chorus of "great meat" at these "informal" chain Americans; the hordes of "casual locals" always find "a friendly face" at these "old-time beefy favorites" where the waitresses "have worked there forever."

Busalacchi's Ristorante S M   23 | 20 | 21 | $27
3683 Fifth Ave. (bet. Brooks & Pennsylvania Sts.), 619-298-0119

■ Pros praise this "enjoyable all-around", "popular red-sauce" Italian "favorite" in Hillcrest that serves "delicious" "traditional Sicilian" standards in a "pleasant setting in an old house"; still, a few detractors dis "uninspired" cooking that "needs more pizazz" and "disinterested service."

Butcher Shop Restaurant M   19 | 15 | 18 | $24
556 Broadway (bet. H & I Sts.), Chula Vista, 619-420-9440 S
5255 Kearny Villa Rd. (bet. Clairemont Mesa Blvd. & Hwy. 163), Kearny Mesa, 619-565-2272

☑ "Testosterone abounds" at these "especially-for-men" steakhouses in Chula Vista and Kearny Mesa that present "extremely good-value" prime rib and steaks in a "tacky", "bordello-like" environment complemented by "easy-on-the-eyes" waitresses who provide "va va va voom" service.

Cafe Athena S M   – | – | – | M
1846 Garnet Ave. (Lamont St.), 619-274-1140
Some of the "best Greek food in SD" can be sampled at this "wholesome" "family place" in Pacific Beach, which offers a "big selection" of "fresh", "homemade" classics like spanakopita; the portions here are large, but the tabs small.

29

Cafe Champagne [S][M] 22 | 21 | 19 | $26

Thornton Winery, 32575 Rancho California Rd. (Butterfield Stage), Temecula, 909-699-0088

◪ "Fabulous food in a dreamy location" is the draw at this "little taste of Napa" at Temecula's Thornton Winery that offers "wonderful" New American choices (don't miss the "scrumptious desserts"); "make reservations to sit outside" on the "lovely" terrace overlooking vine-covered hillsides and linger over "a leisurely lunch" served by a "terrific staff"; but bubble-bursters insist it "should be better" – aside from the "excellent pastries, the rest of the menu is only so-so."

Cafe Eleven [S] 20 | 17 | 19 | $23

Hillcrest Village Sq., 1440 University Ave. (Normal St.), 619-260-8023

■ Find "bargain-of-the-century $9.95 dinner specials" praised as "the best buy in town" for "excellent", if "typical", French fare served in a "cozy atmosphere" at this "great neighborhood restaurant" in Hillcrest; while a few feel this "small place" has "gone downhill a bit", most maintain it serves soups that the "Soup Nazi would envy."

Cafe India [S][M] ▽ 18 | 11 | 18 | $14

Sports Arena Village, 3760-5 Sports Arena Blvd. (Hancock St.), 619-224-7500

■ Even with a minimum of atmosphere and a location in the Sports Arena district that some deem "not ideal", this "best-value" Indian is a "favorite" for its "great veggie buffet" with a "good variety" of items, including some "exotic foods", as well as its refreshing juice bar.

CAFE JAPENGO [S][M] 25 | 24 | 20 | $29

8960 University Ctr. Ln. (bet. La Jolla Village & Lebon Drs.), 619-450-3355

◪ Emphatically "too noisy", this "yuppie heaven" at the epicenter of the Golden Triangle offers "excellent", "artistic sushi" and other Asian-inspired food in an "elegant Japanese setting" that's such a "place to be seen" for singles that those over 30 head to quieter tables in the back; while staffers are "great for viewing", they can be "slow", which fuels critics who say "overrated."

Cafe La Maze [S][M] ▽ 21 | 12 | 18 | $16

1441 Highland Ave. (15th St.), National City, 619-474-3222

■ "Still excellent after all these years" (57 of them), this classic American in the out-of-the-way suburb of National City may be the "best buy in town for great steak" and prime rib; the friendly staff works efficiently in the relaxing atmosphere of an "old, funky" room which a couple of quibblers find "tired and worn"; N.B. there's live entertainment on weekends.

Cafe Luna M
`– – – M`
11040 Rancho Carmel Dr. (east of I-15), 619-673-0077
"A hidden Italian jewel" in Carmel Mountain Ranch, this "cozy, romantic spot" offers a "fabulous" menu that spotlights "outstanding pastas"; the "great" staff is overseen by an amicable owner who doles out "lots of attention."

Cafe on Park S M
`20 15 18 $16`
3831 Park Blvd. (University Ave.), 619-293-7275
■ "You can't go wrong with any of the inexpensive items" at this "wonderful find" in University Heights; order "huge portions" ("enough for three meals!") of "dramatically presented" "phat and phabulous phood" from a "big", "inventive" New American menu.

CAFE PACIFICA S M
`25 22 22 $31`
2414 San Diego Ave. (Old Town Ave.), 619-291-6666
■ "Tremendous seafood" with an "innovative" edge is the specialty of this "consistently strong" performer on the border of historic Old Town, which "never disappoints" the knowledgeable locals and tourists who come here for "great sunsets" and a well-priced menu that draws on solid Californian cuisine traditions; while undeniably "charming", it "could use more space around the tables."

Cafe 222 S M ⊘
`21 17 19 $11`
222 Island Ave. (2nd Ave.), 619-236-9902
■ "If you don't mind waiting", this "perfect neighborhood corner cafe" Downtown cooks up "seriously" "creative and yummy breakfasts" – the "best green eggs and Spam" and "fresh, terrific waffles"; at lunchtime, this "cute, little place" presents an "interesting menu" of "eclectic" Modern Californian interpretations; despite a "lousy location", the smitten "go often" and only "wish they'd open for dinner."

Cafe Zinc S M ⊘
`21 18 16 $13`
132 S. Cedros Ave. (bet. Lomas Santa Fe & Via de la Valle), Solana Beach, 619-793-5436
◪ "Almost hidden" in the suddenly hot design district in Solana Beach, this casual Californian-Vegetarian offers a "beautiful, tree-shaded patio" that's "wonderful for breakfast" (the huevos rancheros are house favorites) and "just as enjoyable in the afternoon" for a lunch of "excellent sandwiches", "creative" four-salad samplers or daily-changing soups; N.B. they don't serve dinner.

Cafe Zucchero S M
`23 20 20 $16`
1731 India St. (Date St.), 619-531-1731
■ The sweet-toothed "love the gelati" and Sicilian pastries at this "delightful" "slice of Italy" with "lots of character" in Little Italy; a "great addition" to the area, with a "friendly" atmosphere, the bakery/cafe also offers a "limited menu of tasty" sandwiches (built with housemade breads), pizzas, salads and entrees at affordable prices.

California Bistro [S] [M] 22 | 25 | 22 | $28

Four Seasons Resort Aviara, 7100 Four Seasons Point (bet. Aviara Pkwy. & Poinsettia Ln.), Carlsbad, 760-603-6868

◪ At this "cheery" room in the "gorgeous" Four Seasons Resort Aviara in posh Carlsbad, the "country French decor", "beautiful" terrace and "wonderful atmosphere" win raves; supporters among the low-key, "stylish crowd" praise the "luxurious" dining experience afforded by "creative" Californian bistro cuisine and a "wonderful" staff; detractors, however, dismiss it as typical hotel dining, though they concede that "ordering from the menu is much preferable to the elaborate yet overrated buffet."

California Cafe Bar & Grill [S] [M] 20 | 20 | 18 | $22

Horton Plaza, 502 Horton Plaza (bet. 1st & 4th Aves.), 619-238-5440

◪ "Convenient when Downtown", this spacious, "bustling" Californian is "surprisingly good for a mall restaurant", offering a "marvelous selection" of "fresh, flavorful and colorful" dishes ("great appetizers and pasta specials"), as well as "excellent wine dinners" at "good value"; even if "the food falls short of spectacular", many shoppers find it "a welcome respite" with a "pretty room" and a popular patio; N.B. there's live Latin jazz on Sundays.

CALIFORNIA CUISINE [S] 24 | 20 | 23 | $28

1027 University Ave. (10th Ave.), 619-543-0790

■ "We never get tired of going back" to this "all-around great" Hillcrest Californian "favorite" with "wonderfully creative combinations on the menu" that are "well-executed" and "imaginatively presented"; the already "sophisticated" setting with a "romantic atmosphere" is now even more so, since there's an exquisite, newly-remodeled garden patio tucked away in the back – a "lovely spot for lovers" that's "fit for proposing."

California Pizza Kitchen [S] [M] 18 | 15 | 17 | $15

11602 Carmel Mtn. Rd. (Rancho Carmel Dr.), Carmel Mtn. Ranch, 619-675-4424

La Jolla Village Sq., 3363 Nobel Dr. (bet. I-5 & Villa La Jolla Dr.), La Jolla, 619-457-4222

Beachwalk, 437 S. Coast Hwy. 101 (bet. Lomas Santa Fe Dr. & Via de la Valle), Solana Beach, 619-793-0999

◪ Somewhat surprisingly, the "great salads" (especially the "best" toss with barbecued chicken and the "tasty" chopped salad) receive as many comments as the "consistently yummy" "novelty pizzas" at these chain emporiums that attract families who enjoy the "satisfying" "fun food" as much as the "good value" and "efficient service"; be warned, though, of "austere", "too-bright" decor and lots of "noise."

Callahan's Pub & Brewery S M
17 | 16 | 17 | $13

Mira Mesa Mall, 8280-A Mira Mesa Blvd. (Camino Ruiz St.), 619-578-7892

■ The grub at this "authentic Irish" brewpub hidden away in the Mira Mesa Mall is "decent" – "ok sandwiches" and "wings of fire" – but the young, local crowd gathers mostly for the "great beers" and "friendly atmosphere"; N.B. Irish folk entertainment is offered on Saturday nights.

Canora's India Street Sandwich Shop S M
16 | 4 | 11 | $8

3715 India St. (Washington St.), 619-291-5938

■ "A good, quick stop" if "you're in Mission Hills", this "favorite sandwich shop" offers one of "the best selections in town" ("try the grilled San Franciscan"), not to mention "generous portions" and cheap prices; the decor leaves everything to be desired, however, so think takeout.

Carino's S M
20 | 12 | 17 | $13

7408 La Jolla Blvd. (Pearl & Marine Sts.), La Jolla, 619-459-1400

■ Ignore the "ugly" "picnic-table decor" at this "longtime neighborhood favorite" in La Jolla and just *mangia* on "excellent", "thin-crust pizzas (like in New York)" that some rate the "best in San Diego"; a "surfer's institution" with a "great" laid-back atmosphere and pleasant staff, this "joint" is definitely "not for snobs."

Casa De Bandini S M
17 | 22 | 17 | $17

2754 Calhoun St. (bet. Taylor & Twiggs Sts.), 619-297-8211

■ Given its location on a busy corner of historic Old Town, it's unsurprising that the clientele of this "beautiful", "colorful" Mexican is "a bit touristy"; even if the menu veers towards "Americanized" "standards", the "huge margaritas", upbeat mood and live mariachi music make this a "fun place to go with a group" of amigos.

Casa de Pico S M
18 | 21 | 17 | $16

Bazaar del Mundo, 2754 Calhoun St. (Twiggs St.), 619-296-3267

◪ "Festive, crowded" and home of margaritas "humongous" "enough to swim in", this popular Mexican (sister to Casa De Bandini) set in an attractive house in Old Town serves "solid" cooking that strikes some as "tourist" fare, but for those who endure "long waits to get in", the "good, cheap eats" and "wonderful atmosphere" are "always a pleasure."

Casa Guadalajara S M
16 | 18 | 15 | $16

4105 Taylor St. (Juan St.), 619-295-5111

◪ So "bright and cheery" that "just walking in the door cheers you up", this spacious Mexican on the edge of Old Town earns "an A+ for accommodating large groups" and kudos for its "great" new garden patio and "good happy hour"; critics, though, dismiss it as a "tourist trap" with "average food" and "pretty poor service" – "nobody seems to know what they're doing."

Casa Machado 🅂🅼 ▽ | 13 | 18 | 19 | $13 |

3750 John J. Montgomery Dr. (Aero Dr.), 619-292-4716

☑ "What fun" it is to "watch the planes land" from a window table at this cheap, casual Mexican near Montgomery Field Airport in the commercial Kearny Mesa district that features a "great" south-of-the-border decor; the "bland" dishes on the typical menu, however, draw major complaints.

Cass Street Bar & Grill 🅂🅼🈂 | – | – | – | I |

4612 Cass St. (bet. Felspar St. & Garnet Ave.), 619-270-1320

Jeans or shorts are the uniforms of choice at this "crowded" Pacific Beach grill where the bartenders serve a "wide variety of beer" to an animated audience; while the menu is nominally American, it offers a little bit of everything – "fresh cioppino", "great Philly cheese steak", "the best Oriental chicken salad ever" and "innovative daily specials."

Cecil's Cafe & Fish Market 🅂🅼 | 20 | 19 | 19 | $19 |

5083 Santa Monica Ave. (Abbot St.), Ocean Beach, 619-222-0501

■ For "reliable bistro fare with spectacular views", this "charming" "hangout" in laid-back Ocean Beach is "one of our absolute favorites", making it "worth the wait"; a "nice, little spot for simple, fast food" – fish tacos, pizza, pastas – it also serves one of the "best breakfasts in town."

Celadon 🅼 | 20 | 19 | 19 | $21 |

3628 Fifth Ave. (bet. Brookes & Pennsylvania Aves.),
619-295-8800

■ "A must-try is the whole, spicy fish", as is "the best green tea ice cream", at this "quiet, pretty, tasteful and tasty" Hillcrest Thai that's watched over by "gracious hosts"; a word of caution: the kitchen doesn't stint on the heat, so even those who like it fiery find some of the "clean and lean" appetizers and entrees "too hot."

Cerveceria Santa Fe 🅼 | 19 | 17 | 16 | $17 |

600 W. Broadway (India St.), 619-696-0043

☑ As the only eatery Downtown that offers "Baja California–style seafood" – "fresh" and "authentic" (the "fish tacos are delicious") – this "informal" Mexican with a "convenient location" on the trolley line can be "noisy", especially during happy hour, which is when the "inconsistent service" becomes "almost nonexistent"; still, many find the house specialties "good for a change" of pace.

Charlie's by the Sea 🅂🅼 | 18 | 20 | 19 | $26 |

2526 S. Coast Hwy. 101 (Cardiff Restaurant Row), Cardiff-by-the-Sea, 760-942-1300

☑ "The food can be disappointing but never the ocean view" at this handsome Californian in Cardiff-by-the-Sea, where the "wonderful beach setting" might compensate for the mostly "uninspired" cuisine; still, the lively bar is "a great place for drinks" and the room is "comfortable", making it for some, "our local favorite" "for seafood and a sunset."

Chart House 🆂Ⓜ   18 | 21 | 18 | $27
525 E. Harbor Dr. (8th Ave.), 619-233-7391
2588 S. Coast Hwy. 101 (bet. Birmingham & Lomas Santa Fe Sts.), Cardiff-by-the-Sea, 760-436-4044
1701 Strand Way (opp. Hotel Del Coronado), Coronado, 619-435-0155
1270 Prospect St. (bet. Girard Ave. & Torrey Pines Rd.), La Jolla, 619-459-8201
314 Harbor Dr. (I-5), Oceanside, 760-722-1345
◪ Boasting some of "the best views" around, the local outlets of this steak-and-seafood chain are "in the best locations", which, alas, "overwhelm the food and service"; while the "beef is reliably good", if "predictable", the seafood is "disappointingly" "mediocre"; those who feel "you've seen one, you've seen them all" think it's "strictly for tourists", but with "always pleasant" environments, defenders say the "old formula still works for me."

Chateau Orleans Ⓜ   19 | 17 | 18 | $21
926 Turquoise St. (Cass St.), Pacific Beach, 619-488-6744
◪ "Hot, spicy" and "decent Cajun" is the draw at this newly remodeled "taste of New Orleans" in Pacific Beach with "campy" decor; while some find the fare "yummy" ("great blackened catfish"), naysayers say it "makes a nice try" but "misses"; the live blues draws mixed reactions too: reviewers either "love the music with dinner" or complain that it makes it "too noisy when dining."

Chez Loma 🆂Ⓜ   21 | 20 | 22 | $32
1132 Loma Ave. (Orange Ave.), Coronado, 619-435-0661
◪ "One of our favorite romantic dinner spots", this "lovely, special-occasion" Continental–New French set in an "intimate", "quaint cottage" ranks "among the best places in Coronado"; regulars praise it as "a gourmet's delight" with "tasty dishes" (including "the best chocolate dessert ever") and "great wines", but skeptics cite "inconsistent quality" and "indifferent service" (the "staff needs polish").

Chilango's 🆂Ⓜ   20 | 8 | 13 | $12
142 University Ave. (bet. 1st & 3rd Aves.), 619-294-8646
▇ "*Muy sabrosa*", enthuse aficionados of this "cramped" Hillcrest grill that's popular for its "interesting variations on a Mexican theme" – "well-prepared", "authentic, regional fast food with character"; sure, it's "a dump" and the speedy servers behind the counter offer "no explanations" about the "unusual" items, but it's "cheap and good."

China Camp at Fat City 🆂Ⓜ   17 | 19 | 17 | $16
2137 Pacific Hwy. (Hawthorn St.), 619-232-0686
◪ The "unique" (or is it "cheesy"?) 19th-century California "mining camp" decor of this long-standing Chinese north of Downtown contributes to its "fun atmosphere", though some think "they could stand to modernize"; sharper criticism is reserved for the fare, which while "reasonable", is only "ok."

China Inn [S] [M] 20 | 14 | 18 | $13

877 Hornblend St. (bet. Garnet & Grand Aves.), 619-483-6680

■ Even if this "best-value" Chinese in the commercial heart of Pacific Beach "looks like a diner", it "fills a need at the beach" by offering "always good" food (try the "ants climbing the tree" concoction) served in "generous portions" by "dependable waiters"; the menu is "extensive", if rather "ordinary, but the chef will prepare special items."

Chino at E Street Alley ▽ 20 | 20 | 17 | $25

919 Fourth Ave. (E St.), 619-231-9200

■ "Stick to the sushi and you'll have a good time" advise fans of this glitzy Asian–New American attached to a basement-level Gaslamp nightclub; the "young crowd" "eats at the bar", enjoying "awesome" raw fish; the rest of the menu is "ok", but "overwhelmed by the snazzy decor."

Chu Dynasty [S] [M] ▽ 17 | 12 | 17 | $17

1033 B Ave. (Orange Ave.), Coronado, 619-435-5300

◪ After 26 years as the principal Chinese in Coronado, some feel it's "getting tired", if not already "long in the tooth"; but pros say that the food is still "good" enough (the "Peking duck is excellent"), reasonably priced and promptly served.

Chuey's Numero Uno [S] [M] 20 | 18 | 20 | $12

1894 Main St. (Crosby St.), 619-234-6937

■ As the "quintessential Downtown Mexican hangout" for a "high-powered clientele of local politicians, lawyers" and "movers and shakers", this colorful, "old-time" "tradition" housed in a Quonset hut in Barrio Logan serves "authentic California-Mexican cuisine" – "great shrimp ranchero", "great hot sauce", "great everything"; a "favorite" inexpensive "standby", this lively "place has soul."

Cilantros [S] [M] 21 | 20 | 20 | $26

3702 Via de la Valle (Camino Real Rd.), Del Mar, 619-259-8777

◪ Frequented by "beautiful" "polo people" from the nearby Del Mar grounds and other "trendies", this "upscale" Southwestern "with polish" ("Tex-Mex with a top hat") turns out "dynamite food" – "always innovative" and "flavorful"; on the negative side, "portions are small", the "noise level is absurd" and service varies wildly from "attentive" to "poor."

Cindy Black's [S] 22 | 18 | 21 | $33

5721 La Jolla Blvd. (Bird Rock Ave.), La Jolla, 619-456-6299

◪ An "all-around winner", this Contemporary French in the Bird Rock neighborhood of La Jolla "always satisfies" with "superb fare" prepared by "talented" chef Cindy Black (everybody raves about the "delicious soft-shell crabs" in season) and served in a "comfortable", "quiet atmosphere"; critics find it "overpriced for standard Nouvelle stuff" and complain that "some dishes are getting old" ("the menu needs an overhaul"); not many, however, complain about the "prix fixe Sunday menu", which is "a total bargain."

City Delicatessen & Bakery ●🅂🅼   16 | 13 | 16 | $12
535 University Ave. (6th St.), 619-295-2747
☑ The "only decent place open late" in Hillcrest (or just about anywhere in San Diego), this "stuck-in-time" Jewish deli dishes out the "best stuffed cabbage in town", "hearty, no-nonsense sandwiches" and "good smoked fish"; purists sniff a "NYC-style deli, my foot", but "the right prices", "friendly waiters and a relaxed atmosphere" keep this noshery "always crowded."

Claim Jumper 🅂🅼   18 | 18 | 18 | $17
5958 Avenida Encinas (bet. I-5 & Palomar Airport Rd.), Carlsbad, 760-431-0889
12384 Carmel Mtn. Rd. (Rancho Carmel Drive), Carmel Mtn. Ranch, 619-485-8370
Grossmont Ctr., 5500 Grossmont Ctr. Dr. (Murray Dr.), La Mesa, 619-469-3927
☑ Welcome to "pigoutsville" where the "obscenely" "huge portions" ("I dare you to eat it all") of "manly grub" draw "noisy", "family-oriented" crowds to this American BBQ chain (voted tops in SD); there's "good ribs and chicken", but for those on "a health kick", there's a surprisingly impressive salad bar; though these "carnivores' delights" are "bargains", detractors counter that the "monstrous gobs of food are as bland as they are big."

Cody's 🅂🅼   – | – | – | I
8030 Girard Ave. (bet. Coast Blvd. & Prospect St.), La Jolla, 619-459-0040
Boasting perhaps the most affordable ocean view in La Jolla, this New American newcomer packs in cost-conscious locals who breakfast on the Hangtown Fry (a tasty scramble of oysters, eggs and spinach) and lunch on Caesar salad with grilled salmon or a basket of miniburgers.

Come On In! Cafe & Bakery 🅂⊄   25 | 16 | 21 | $11
1030-B Torrey Pines Rd. (Herschel Ave.), La Jolla, 619-551-1063
■ "Everything is homemade" at this "fabulous gourmet secret" where the "bakery smells too good to stay out"; a "jewel of La Jolla", it's a "cozy place" to have breakfast – "superior" pancakes (the "lemon soufflé stack is heavenly") and waffles – and it's a "delightful lunch spot" too; a "staff that pays wonderful attention to the customers" makes this Californian the "perfect neighborhood cafe."

Corvette Diner 🅂🅼   17 | 23 | 20 | $15
3946 Fifth Ave. (bet. University Ave. & Washington St.), 619-542-1476
■ At this "high energy" Hillcrest diner, the Elvis era lives on with a "great '50s atmosphere", DJs and "campy" service that's "a show", delighting kids and making it "the most fun place around" for parties; the "home cooking"–style eats run the likes of "greasy but fab" hamburgers and the "best shakes"; it's "a formula, but it works."

Cottage, The [S] [M] 21 | 21 | 21 | $15

7702 Fay Ave. (Kline St.), La Jolla, 619-454-8409

■ It's the "perfect patio for pancakes" purr partisans of this "lovely" La Jolla Californian where "hordes" of "casual" locals also come to savor "excellent omelets" and "good cinnamon rolls", and later in the day, an "imaginative", if "limited", lunch menu ("fabulous Jamaican shrimp salad"); "the owner makes [diners] feel welcome" and the staff is "friendly", so it's "always a pleasant experience"; N.B. dinner is served May 15–October 15.

Coyote Bar & Grill [S] [M] 18 | 19 | 18 | $17

Village Faire, 300 Carlsbad Village Dr. (Carlsbad Blvd.), Carlsbad, 760-729-4695

◪ "Loud but fun" because of the "great live music", this Southwestern "hangout" for "young adults" in Carlsbad features "unique" decor; while the food may be "ordinary", it's a "good pickup joint."

Crab Catcher [S] [M] 19 | 21 | 18 | $25

1298 Prospect St. (bet. Cave St. & Ivanhoe Ave.), La Jolla, 619-454-9587

◪ Perched "high over La Jolla Cove", this "scenic" seafooder with a "beautiful setting" draws praise from some for its "fresh fish" delivered by an "attentive" staff; those "not impressed", however, criticize the "service that varies with the waiter" and the "disappointing menu of plain food" that's "not up to the" "stunning ocean view."

Crescent Shores Grill [S] [M] 18 | 23 | 17 | $34

Hotel La Jolla, 7955 La Jolla Shores Dr. (Torrey Pines Rd.), La Jolla, 619-459-0541

◪ "Go for a drink and enjoy the view" of the shoreline suggest those who have sampled the New American cuisine at this hotel-topper in La Jolla; the "ambitious kitchen" boasts "inventive cooking", but the results are "wildly uneven" and the service is similarly "spotty"; some surveyors say the grill "lacks the presence of management" and many feel the menu "needs work to be worthy" of its "spectacular" location.

Crest Cafe ◐ [S] [M] 19 | 13 | 19 | $13

425 Robinson Ave. (bet. 4th & 5th Aves.), 619-295-2510

■ "If you need a fat, greasy burger now", head to this inexpensive, "dependable" Hillcrest American with "fast, friendly waiters" working a "tiny" room that's short on looks ("redo that decor!"), but is "never disappointing"; a "homey" "neighborhood institution", it's "one of our favorites" for "diner food good" enough (the "best onion loaf") to draw the lively crowd that "keeps this place hopping."

Croce's Restaurant ◗ⓈⓂ   17 | 17 | 17 | $25
802 Fifth Ave. (F St.), 619-233-4355

☑ Operated by pop singer Jim Croce's widow, this "entertaining" SW eatery/jazz club in the Gaslamp Quarter is "fun, fun, fun for a late-night music spot", but respondents go "more for the jazz", which is "wonderful", "than for the food", which swings from "great" to "not as good as in the past"; despite "indifferent", sometimes "rude" service, "if you're young and want to be hip, come here."

Crocodile Cafe ⓈⓂ   17 | 18 | 18 | $16
Fashion Valley Mall, 7007 Friars Rd. (Fashion Valley Rd.), 619-297-3247

☑ A "safe bet if you're already at the mall", this "pleasant" Mission Valley Californian offers "yuppies" a convenient "break from shopping" with an "unusual" menu that can be "surprisingly good" – "we love the fried bananas" and the "great ahi sandwich" – delivered by a "well-trained staff"; while the decor is "cheerful", skeptics "wish the food spoke as loudly as the room."

Crown Room ⓈⓂ   21 | 25 | 21 | $33
Hotel del Coronado, 1500 Orange Ave. (R. H. Dana Pl.), Coronado, 619-522-8888

☑ "Regal and classy", this "enormous", "one-of-a-kind room in a one-of-a-kind hotel" is renowned as "a special-occasion dinner-and-dancing" destination, as well as the site of a "great Sunday brunch"; while loyalists like the "good" Continental cuisine, critics call it "basic", but admit the room's "elegance seems to make the food taste better."

Daily's ⓈⓂ   21 | 13 | 17 | $11
Renaissance Towne Ctr., 8915 Towne Ctr. Dr. (bet. La Jolla Village & Nobel Drs.), 619-453-1112

■ Since "they make healthy food taste good", "what more can you ask?" (except to have them open "more locations") wonder grateful partisans of this Golden Triangle fast-fooder; this popular "good idea" turns out "fresh", "delicious" "low-calorie meals" – the "ginger Thai noodles are a standout" and the "veggie burger is the best in town"; the "too-minimalist" room could certainly be "made more comfy", but for a "no-guilt" "bargain", this is a "favorite."

Dakota Grill & Spirits ⓈⓂ   21 | 21 | 19 | $24
901 Fifth Ave. (E St.), 619-234-5554

☑ The "trendy crowd" that jams this "creatively decorated" Southwestern grill in the Gaslamp Quarter generates an "energizing" atmosphere that's "good for people-watching"; the kitchen "makes the basics outstanding" with "nice spice", and desserts rate a special "wow" (try the signature chocolate pecan torte); while some feel it's "better for lunch than dinner", others find it a "reliable nightspot", despite the "deafening piano music", but those who call it a "has-been" just say "zzzz."

39

Dao Son Noodle House 🅢🅜   –|–|–| I

2322 El Cajon Blvd. (Texas St.), 619-291-5051

Because the Japanese "noodles are always good" and cheap, regulars forgive the "ugly" setting of this tiny North Park joint and don't much mind the no-nonsense service either; many also praise the "outstanding Vietnamese homestyle" cooking, though a few feel that the "food used to be better."

DELICIAS 🅜   25 | 26 | 24 | $36

6106 Paseo Delicias (La Granada), Rancho Santa Fe, 619-756-8000

■ "Fresh flowers" and "beautiful" country French decor serve as the backdrop for an equally good-looking crowd at this "cozy", "comfortable" Californian in the heart of wealthy Rancho Santa Fe; while the "warm, intimate" ambiance attracts the most comments, high ratings also go to the "excellent" food and "careful" service; in sum, it's "worth a visit", especially for lunch.

De Luca's Ristorante 🅢🅜   19 | 16 | 18 | $20

228 W. Washington St. (bet. Albatross & Front Sts.), 619-220-7070

☑ It's "so cute and quaint" gush those who find this "excellent neighborhood" Hillcrest Italian an "authentic gem", due to "great portions" of "well-prepared" "basics" ("wonderful chicken parmigiana" and lasagna), a "casual, homey atmosphere" and "good-value" prices; even if the "widely variable service" (they "need more waiters") gives some "the feeling that the place is disorganized", the "interesting lunch buffet" keeps locals streaming in.

de Medici 🅢🅜   20 | 22 | 19 | $31

815 Fifth Ave. (bet. E & F Sts.), 619-702-7228

☑ The "Renaissance setting" of this "attractive, upscale" Italian seafooder makes it "a Gaslamp Quarter treat" say admirers who "love the opera-singing waiters", "the maitre d' who makes things special" and the "standout" "regional food" that's "just like mama's cooking"; however, cynics sniff that it makes "an attempt at class", but "just misses."

Di-Chan 🅢🅜   –|–|–| I

Madison Sq. Ctr., 5535 Clairemont Mesa Blvd. (west of I-805), 619-569-0084

"Consistently good Thai" and a willingness to prepare "special orders" make this "very nice", inexpensive "neighborhood place" in a commercial corner of Clairemont popular; the service is sometimes "challenged", but the "food and warmth from the great owner compensate."

Dick's Last Resort ◐ [S] [M] — 11 | 13 | 12 | $16
345 Fourth Ave. (bet. J & K Sts.), 619-231-9100
◪ "Cheesy" by design, this "outrageously" "wild and crazy" "huge greasy spoon" in the Gaslamp Quarter is "rowdy" and "crude", with "bras over the bar" and "toilet paper on the floor"; "the draw" is an "obnoxious", "mouthy staff" that "insults" diners – all in the name of "entertainment" (though some say they're "not as funny as they think"); the "too ordinary" American BBQ is an afterthought for most, who come more to "kick back to the [live] music."

Dining Room, The [S] [M] — 23 | 23 | 23 | $33
L'Auberge Del Mar Resort & Spa, 1540 Camino Del Mar (15th St.), Del Mar, 619-793-6460
■ "Get a name" wryly suggest some gourmands regarding this "elegant" room at Del Mar's tony L'Auberge resort; nonetheless, there's praise for the "exceptional service" and "wonderful" California wine country–inspired menu, including perhaps "the best prix fixe early-bird specials in the country", as well a "fabulous breakfast outside" on the "delightful patio."

Dini's by the Sea [S] [M] — 15 | 15 | 17 | $18
Tamarack Beach Resort, 3290 Carlsbad Blvd. (Walnut Rd.), Carlsbad, 760-434-6000
◪ A "wonderful place for a sunset" rather than riveting food, this midpriced American seafooder in Carlsbad sports a "pleasant seaside setting" with a lovely view.

D'Lish Bistro [S] [M] — 18 | 14 | 17 | $15
2260 Otay Lakes Rd. (Eastlake Pkwy.), 619-216-3900
Terra Nova Shopping Ctr., 386 E. H St. (I-805 S.), Chula Vista, 619-585-1371
7514 Girard Ave. (Pearl St.), La Jolla, 619-459-8118
■ "Lively" and "reliable", these chain Internationals are "fun neighborhood places that are good for kids"; the kitchen turns "tasty, fresh ingredients into pleasing" "designer pizzas", pastas and salads; even with sometimes "unfriendly" service, the "huge portions" at "nice-value" prices make this trio a "favorite choice."

DOBSON'S [M] — 25 | 21 | 23 | $32
956 Broadway Circle (2nd Ave.), 619-231-6771
■ "Rub shoulders with the Downtown power group" at this "clubby", "cosmopolitan" "hangout" with a "real city feel" that's "choice for business lunches" and also "a grand place before the theater"; "too cramped", "crowded" and "expensive", it wins kudos aplenty anyway for its "always terrific", "exciting" New American menu (the "mussel bisque is outstanding"), "sophisticated" service and "the best owner-host in the city, Paul Dobson – nothing escapes his notice."

Downtown Johnny Brown's S M   17 | 14 | 15 | $12
Civic Ctr. Concourse, 1220 Third Ave. (B St.), 619-232-8414
■ A "blazer-wearing after-work crowd mixes with a tuxedo-wearing pre-opera crowd" at this cheap, "noisy" "fun spot Downtown" near the Civic Theater; a "comfortable sports bar" boasting a "pub-like atmosphere" and "great beer and burgers", it's "good to meet friends for drinks" here, but "don't expect much service."

D.Z. Akin's S M   22 | 13 | 19 | $14
6930 Alvarado Rd. (70th St.), La Mesa, 619-265-0218
■ Voted the top deli in SD, this State College district landmark attracts mobs longing for a "delicious fix" of the "closest thing to authentic NY deli"; the "mmm good" "homestyle Jewish food" is highlighted by "super matzo ball soup", "lox to die for" and "giant sandwiches"; the service may be "crabby", but it's "quick" – "move 'em in, move 'em out."

El Agave S M   22 | 19 | 19 | $25
2304 San Diego Ave. (Old Town Ave.), 619-220-0692
■ For a "nice change from the typical Old Town Mexican", try this "really inventive", "upscale" spot that's celebrated for its "cool tequila selection" ("over 300" choices) and "honest regional cuisine"; though a few mumble it's "overpriced", most find this "outstanding treat" to be "a perfect addition to SD."

EL BIZCOCHO S M   28 | 26 | 26 | $44
Rancho Bernardo Inn, 17550 Bernardo Oaks Dr.
(Rancho Bernardo Rd.), Rancho Bernardo, 619-675-8550
■ The last bastion of black-tie service in San Diego, this grand hotel dining room may be "far, far" from Downtown in Rancho Bernardo, but it takes top honors for its "world-class" Classic and Contemporary French cuisine; the "sublime" service and "elegant decor" add to the appeal, and while it's "pretty pricey" (especially the wine list), most agree the raves are "well-deserved"; P.S. don't overlook the "best brunch" in town.

Elephant Bar S M   15 | 17 | 15 | $15
17051 W. Bernardo Dr. (Rancho Bernardo Rd.), Rancho Bernardo, 619-487-7181
☑ While the La Jolla branch is "history", the Rancho Bernardo outpost of this safari-themed watering hole continues to dish out "good, plain" American fare; some say it's "ok if you're 20" and advise "only go to drink and socialize", but penny-pinchers praise the "great value."

El Fandango S M   13 | 18 | 14 | $14
2734 Calhoun St. (Juan St.), 619-298-2860
☑ Sun worshipers "love to sit on the patio" and enjoy the "nice garden setting" at this affordable, "typical Mexican" in Old Town; still, "slow service" and "gringo food" prompt naysayers to feel "sorry for the tourists who blunder in."

El Indio Shop 🅂Ⓜ
409 F St. (4th Ave.), 619-239-8151
3695 India St. (Washington St.), 619-299-0333
■ "Authentic" "landmarks", these "SD traditions" near Old Town and Downtown offer "good-quality Mexican food" that's "fast and cheap"; granted, there's "no atmosphere" at these "no-frills" joints, but enough enthusiasts would "drive miles for the chips" to keep them "sentimental favorites."

El Ranchero 🅂Ⓜ
▽ 15 | 10 | 15 | $13
7404 La Jolla Blvd. (bet. Marine & Pearl Sts.), La Jolla, 619-459-5877
■ "College kids returning home" make this "favorite dive" their "first stop" for Mexican munchies, and this longtime "institution" (since 1939) is popular with "old-line La Jolla families" too; though it might have "ugly decor", it's a "good local hangout" where "you get what you pay for."

El Tecolote 🅂Ⓜ
17 | 14 | 16 | $14
6110 Friars Rd. W. (Via Las Cumbres), 619-295-2087
🄯 Partisans praise this "family-run" Mission Valley Mexican for "authentic dishes" (the "best mole in town") that are "quickly served" and are "good for children"; but skeptics say it's a "long-established" spot that's "seen better days" and is "not too inspiring."

El Torito 🅂Ⓜ
14 | 16 | 15 | $15
16375 Bernardo Ctr. Dr. (I-15), 619-485-1905
445 Camino del Rio S. (Mission Ctr. Rd.), 619-296-6154
8223 Mira Mesa Blvd. (3 mi. west of I-15), 619-566-5792
271 Bay Blvd. W. (I-5), Chula Vista, 619-425-6013
8910 Villa La Jolla Dr. (La Jolla Village Dr.), La Jolla, 619-453-4115
5024 Baltimore Dr. (El Cajon Blvd.), La Mesa, 619-698-7404
2693 Vista Way (El Camino Real), Oceanside, 760-439-5407
🄯 It might be "kinda touristy", but fans of this "consistent chain" say the Mexican fare is "better than you'd expect"; however, critics counter that it's "Americanized" "food for the masses" and "strictly for East Coast people."

Embers Grille 🅂
20 | 17 | 19 | $17
Midway Towne Ctr., 3924 W. Point Loma Blvd. (Sports Arena Blvd.), 619-222-6877
■ "Reasonable pizzas and pastas" pull them into this "neat" Point Loma Italian grill (a spin-off of the Souplantation chain) that's a "cut above" the competition; "popular with locals", it's "family-friendly" and located near SeaWorld.

EMERALD CHINESE SEAFOOD ◑🅂Ⓜ
24 | 18 | 19 | $21
Pacific Gateway Plaza, 3709 Convoy St. (Aero Dr.), 619-565-6888
■ For a "fantastic variety of dim sum", try this Convoy Street Chinese where "top-of-the-class" fare is prepared "Hong Kong–style"; though this sprawling, 600-seater "can get noisy", diehards delight in the "great fresh seafood."

Emperor's Palace 🇸🇲   — — — M
*Ralph's Shopping Ctr., 11835 Carmel Mtn. Rd. (east of I-15),
619-673-2279*
The kitchen is unusually talented at this traditional Chinese
in suburban Carmel Mountain Ranch, wokking such treats
as shredded pork with onion cake, stir-fried lamb with
scallions and dry-braised scallops; though the lighting is
blindingly bright, the service is somewhat dim.

Epazote 🇸🇲   21 22 18 $23
*Del Mar Plaza, 1555 Camino del Mar (15th St.), Del Mar,
619-259-9966*
■ "Spicy Southwestern succulence" draws crowds to
this "pretty Del Mar" spot with a "priceless view" and a
"trendy crowd", some of whom are there for the "bar
scene" and not necessarily the food; still, defenders praise
the "zippy", "creative menu."

Eric's Ribs & Steak 🇸🇲   13 9 14 $19
4263 Taylor St. (Morena Blvd.), 619-298-4255
☑ At this "old-style" rib joint-cum-steakhouse, the "crispy
onion loaves" make some fans say "mmm", but otherwise,
surveyors find the fare to be "very average"; the "dated
atmosphere" also fails to impress, leaving critics to
conclude you should stop by "only if you're in Old Town
and don't want Mexican" food.

Fairouz Cafe 🇸🇲   19 17 18 $14
Midway Village, 3166 Midway Dr. (Rosecrans St.), 619-225-0308
■ "Don't miss the dinner buffet" – a "tasty Mideastern
smorgasbord" – that lures patrons to this "terrific, little
cafe" in the Midway district; with its "nice veggie" entrees,
good service and "local artwork", it's pretty stylish for an
affordable low-key, "kid-friendly" "neighborhood place."

Fargo's BBQ 🇸   ▽ 21 6 16 $13
6171 Imperial Ave. (bet. 61st & 62nd Sts.), 619-262-0201
■ The "ribs are great, the neighborhood is not" is the
capsule verdict on this decor-free, "out-of-the-way"
Caribbean BBQ shack in East San Diego; "Mrs. Williams
is wonderful" say admirers of the cheerful proprietor and
some rate her "inexpensive" eats the "best Jamaican" in
the city, though realists note there's "not much competition."

Fidel's Little Mexico 🇸🇲   18 16 17 $15
607 Valley Ave. (Genevieve St.), Solana Beach, 619-755-5292
Fidel's Norte 🇸🇲
3003 Carlsbad Blvd. (Carlsbad Village Dr.), Carlsbad, 760-729-0903
☑ "Reliable" and usually "crowded", these "all-time faves
for Mexican" in Solana Beach and Carlsbad satisfy with
midpriced, "good, traditional" items ("heavenly *carnitas*" and
the "best *chile rellenos* in town"); though some detect
"nothing special", regulars enjoy the "lovely seating in the
garden" and anticipate both "a special treat" and "a wait."

44

FIELD, THE [S][M] 20 | 27 | 20 | $15

544 Fifth Ave. (bet. Island Ave. & Market St.), 619-232-9840

■ The "charming", "dark pub atmosphere" is the "strong suit" of this "awesome bar" and Gaelic eatery in the Gaslamp Quarter; "wonderful food and decor", "antiques from Ireland" and servers with "lilting accents" make this a "cool", "terrific addition" and a magnet for a "young crowd" that likens it to "being in Ireland again."

Fifth & Hawthorne [S][M] 22 | 18 | 21 | $25

515 Hawthorne St. (5th Ave.), 619-544-0940

■ Upholding its reputation as a "quiet experience every time" and a "great pre-theater" stop, this Midtown "gem" near Balboa Park delivers with a "creative" American-Californian menu, "cozy" atmosphere and "attentive service"; the "easy-on-the-wallet" prix fixe dinner lets "two dine for $39", with wine.

Filippi's Pizza Grotto [S][M] 19 | 14 | 17 | $13

10330 Friars Rd. (Riverdale St.), 619-281-3511
1747 India St. (Date St.), 619-232-5094
5353 Kearny Villa Rd. (Clairemont Mesa Blvd.), 619-279-7240
9969 Mira Mesa Blvd. (I-15), 619-586-0888
82 Broadway (D St.), Chula Vista, 619-427-6650
114 W. Grand Ave. (Broadway), Escondido, 760-747-2650
962 Garnet Ave. (Cass St.), Pacific Beach, 619-483-6222
13000 Oak Knoll Dr. (Poway Rd.), Poway, 619-748-1800

■ This hometown chain's "Little Italy location" in particular "smells wonderful" and offers among the "best values", making it an "Italian kitsch" "favorite" for "homestyle" cooking, notably "pizza that will make you say *mama mia*"; the "no-frills" decor is a trade-off.

Fins - A Mexican Eatery [S][M] 19 | 12 | 15 | $9

Mission Valley Ctr., 1640 Camino del Rio N., 619-283-3467
Ralph's Shopping Ctr., 9460-H Mira Mesa Blvd. (Westview Pkwy.), 619-549-3467
La Jolla Village Sq., 8657 Villa La Jolla Dr. (Nobel Dr.), La Jolla, 619-270-3467
High Country Plaza, 15817 Bernardo Ctr. Dr. (Camino del Norte), Rancho Bernardo, 619-484-3467

◪ For "speedy, fresh, authentic 'Cal-healthy' Mex", this seafaring chain with "spartan decor" offers "satisfying fast food" of "yummy" burritos and "cool fish tacos"; N.B. no beer at the Rancho Bernardo branch.

Fio's Cucina Italiana [S][M] 22 | 22 | 20 | $30

801 Fifth Ave. (F St.), 619-234-3467

◪ This Gaslamp Quarter stalwart is "reliable and desirable" for "a true Italian experience"; the "attentive service" and "great decor" make it a "special-occasion" and "date place" and its location makes it convenient for dining "before or after the theater"; those who sniff it has "gone a bit downhill of late" are soundly outnumbered.

Firehouse Beach Cafe 🅢🅜   16 | 16 | 16 | $15
722 Grand Ave. (Mission Blvd.), 619-272-1999
☑ An ultracasual clientele "loves dining outside" at this "beach hangout" in Pacific Beach that's a "Bloody Mary heaven" and a fave for "good" Traditional American breakfasts served on a "rooftop sundeck with a view" of the ocean; the "relaxing" mood and reasonable prices pull in a lively evening crowd too, despite the "average bar food" served at night.

Firenze Trattoria 🅢🅜   21 | 20 | 22 | $26
West Village, 162 S. Rancho Santa Fe Rd. (bet. Encinitas Blvd. & Manchester Ave.), Encinitas, 760-944-9000
■ Tucked away in the Encinitas backcountry, this Italian "dream place to eat" has "a reputation for quality cuisine"; regulars go for the "enjoyable", if sometimes "loud", setting and "good" service, not to mention the "excellent value."

Fish House Vera Cruz 🅢🅜   19 | 17 | 17 | $19
417 Carlsbad Village Dr. (I-5), Carlsbad, 760-434-6777
360 Via Vera Cruz (San Marcos Blvd.), San Marcos, 760-744-8000
■ "Sensible fish and low prices" are the lures at these Carlsbad and San Marcos twins; the mesquite-grilled "quality seafood" tops off a menu with "lots of choices" ("love the cheesy potatoes" and the "salad with smoked albacore is to die for"); "good-sized portions" also ensure that families and "retirees love it."

FISH MARKET, THE 🅢🅜   22 | 19 | 19 | $23
2316 Poinsettia Dr. (bet. Broadway & Pacific Hwy.), 619-232-3474
640 Via de la Valle (Jimmy Durante Blvd.), Solana Beach, 619-755-2277
■ The Downtown flagship of this mariner minichain offers "a nice view from the deck" to complement the "outstanding variety" of "dependably fresh", "excellent seafood" from a menu some proclaim is "for fish lovers only"; enthusiastic locals and conventioneers create an "always bustling" atmosphere that works best "if you like your fish noisy."

Fish Merchant 🅢🅜   19 | 16 | 18 | $19
7005 Navajo Rd. (Jackson Dr.), 619-462-3811
☑ Partisans commend the "fresh seafood" at this San Carlos "neighborhood family" entry; more cautious types say the "fish is always good but not exceptional", in keeping with the "simple" style of this "casual place."

Forever Fondue 🅢🅜   ▽ 19 | 12 | 18 | $21
1295 Prospect St. (Cave St.), La Jolla, 619-551-4509
☑ Surveyors concur that this "one-of-a-kind" La Jolla fondue house is "different"; but whether that means the eating experience here is "fun" or "strange" will have to be your call.

Fortune Cookie Restaurant 🆂Ⓜ – | – | – | M
16425 Bernardo Center Dr. (east of I-15), Rancho Bernardo, 619-451-8958
Admirers rank this "delightful" Rancho Bernardo winner the "best Chinese in the area", thanks to a "large menu" of multiregional fare that's "consistently" executed and served by a superlative staff in a sophisticated, "upscale setting."

French Gourmet, The 🆂Ⓜ 21 | 14 | 18 | $21
960 Turquoise St. (bet. Cass St. & Mission Blvd.), Pacific Beach, 619-488-1725
✇ Though the "bistro atmosphere" may be a little unpolished at this "delightful" Pacific Beach "old soft shoe", most declare that the "good French food" "overcomes the decor"; it's "dependable for a simple meal" note fans who especially "love the bakery's" "great desserts."

French Market Grille 🆂Ⓜ 24 | 21 | 20 | $27
15717 Bernardo Hts. Pkwy. (Pomerado Rd.), Rancho Bernardo, 619-485-8055
■ The "freshest ingredients" help make a "real French food heaven" of this "distinctive" and "romantic" Rancho Bernardo "European-American bistro"; the "nice patio" attracts well-heeled locals who dub it an "excellent little find" for "gourmet yet casual" dining.

Gathering, The 🆂Ⓜ 14 | 14 | 16 | $16
902 W. Washington St. (Goldfinch St.), 619-260-0400
✇ Did this Hillcrest "local favorite" "take a dive when it moved across the street" or does it hold up as a nifty "neighborhood gathering place"?; though opinions are split on the "consistent", if uninspired, American food, regulars call it a "friendly" hangout.

GEORGE'S AT THE COVE 🆂Ⓜ 26 | 26 | 25 | $37
1250 Prospect St. (bet. Cave & Ivanhoe Sts.), La Jolla, 619-454-4244
■ This "real La Jolla tradition" is again voted San Diego's Most Popular restaurant, thanks to "impressive" New American fare from chef Scott Meskan and a triple-tiered setting offering "romantic", "less expensive" dining "on the roof under a full moon", a pricier ground-floor main room that "can't miss for business" meals and a bar in between; if "hospitable" host George is around, it's even easier to see why this place is "consistently on top."

Georgia's Greek Cuisine 🆂Ⓜ ▽ 18 | 13 | 18 | $15
3550 Rosecrans St. (bet. Midway Dr. & Sports Arena Blvd.), 619-523-1007
✇ Serving what some say are the "No. 1 dolmades", this moderately priced Greek in the Midway district is also favored by connoisseurs of souvlaki and "terrific rice pudding" who can forgive "not-impressive decor" because it plates up "lots of food."

Girard Gourmet 🅂Ⓜ⇗   _-_ | _-_ | _-_ | I

7837 Girard Ave. (Silverado St.), La Jolla, 619-454-3321
Find this delectable gourmet deli/Belgian bakery in La Jolla
just by looking for the noontime line stretching down chic
Girard Avenue; drawing cards include "great sandwiches"
on housemade bread, "stellar cookies and Danish" pastries
and what many consider the "best soups anywhere."

Grant Grill 🅂Ⓜ   23 | 24 | 23 | $35

U.S. Grant Hotel, 326 Broadway (bet. 3rd & 4th Aves.),
619-232-3121
■ "One of the best places to impress a client", this
"beautifully appointed" hotel dining room in the heart of
Downtown is celebrated for "top-drawer" Californian-French
cuisine, "good, old-fashioned service" and a "New Yorky,"
"private-club mood" that some find "stiff" but most "love"; a
"pricey" "classic", it's patronized by a dressy crowd that
tends to converse in murmurs.

Great Wall Cafe 🅂Ⓜ   ▽ 13 | 11 | 14 | $15

2543 Congress St. (Twiggs St.), 619-291-9478
◪ This Szechuan specialist in a quiet corner of Old Town
offers a "good deal" on "ok" chow and though there's
"better Chinese around", some are hooked, declaring it
"worth multiple visits"; those in the know advise "watch
the weather, as most seating is outdoors" on a broad,
partly sheltered terrace.

Greek Town Restaurant 🅂   ▽ 17 | 17 | 13 | $15

431 E St. (bet. 4th & 5th Aves.), 619-232-0461
■ "Try the lemon chicken" at this informal and lively "family"
Greek in the Gaslamp Quarter, where a boisterous crowd
assembles for the "great, fun atmosphere" and cheap,
generously portioned traditional cooking.

Green Flash, The 🅂Ⓜ   15 | 17 | 18 | $17

701 Thomas Ave. (bet. Mission & Ocean Blvds.), Pacific
Beach, 619-270-7715
◪ "The people-watching is great" and the "breakfasts are
abundant and tasty" at this Californian "hangout" on the
boardwalk in Pacific Beach; while the "great location" is
"fun for brunch" and patrons praise it for "surprisingly good"
seafood, a minority maintains it's a "waste of great potential",
unless what you're interested in is "beer and babes."

Guava Beach Bar & Grill ❶🅂Ⓜ ▽ 16 | 19 | 16 | $16

3714 Mission Blvd. (Santa Clara Pl.), Mission Beach,
619-488-6688
◪ A "good place to end a day at the beach", this "little" spot
in Mission Beach features a "comfortable atmosphere"
enhanced by "friendly employees" and a Mexican–Pacific
Rim menu that strikes some as "interesting"; while skeptics
think it "used to be better", the mostly young clientele has
made it a "laid-back" refuge.

Gulf Coast Grill S M

— | — | — | M

4130 Park Blvd. (Polk Ave.), 619-295-2244

"Exciting Gulf Coast cuisine – a little Creole, a little Cajun, a little Southern", along with accents from Mexico's Gulf of California – is showcased at this "great new place" in Hillcrest that specializes in "yummy" seafood courtesy of chef Victor Jimenez; its attractive setting, "terrifically" enhanced by the artwork splashed on the walls, appeals to an eclectic crowd who relishes the unusual menu.

Gumbo Pot, The S

▽ 13 | 10 | 11 | $17

Westwood Ctr., 11655 Duenda Rd. (W. Bernardo Rd.), 619-673-3850

☑ Pros praise the crab cakes and the "tangy, smoky and spicy jambalaya" at this decor-resistant, Louisiana-style joint in a Rancho Bernardo mall; but doubters find it "disappointing", challenging "if this be Cajun, prove it!" – "thank goodness it was cheap."

Hamburger Mary's S M

18 | 16 | 16 | $13

308 University Ave. (bet. 3rd & 4th Sts.), 619-491-0400

■ This "festive and fun" Hillcrest entry features an all-American menu with "tasty hamburgers", hot wings and a "great veggie burger"; "open and inviting", it's a "popular gay hangout" with outdoor seating for "people-watching", which earns it bonus points among those who already "love the food."

Hang Ten Brewing Co. S M

16 | 15 | 17 | $15

310 Fifth Ave. (bet. J & K Sts.), 619-232-6336

☑ "The Downtown surf bar" of the moment, this American BBQ at the southern edge of the Gaslamp Quarter "takes me back to the '60s, dude", attracting young and noisy revelers with "great beers" brewed on the premises and "fair food" that some find "surprisingly good for a tourist" draw; the quieter patio is a refuge for those "too old for beer blasts."

Harbor House S M

19 | 20 | 18 | $23

Sea Port Village, 831 W. Harbor Dr. (Pacific Hwy.), 619-232-1141

☑ "Try the filet mignon and the view" advise supporters of this surf 'n' turf specialist, which boasts a "lovely" harbor vista and "pretty good food"; located in Seaport Village on the Downtown waterfront, it tends to be "touristic", but the steaks and fish are "satisfying" and the "pleasant" service makes for smooth dining.

Hard Rock Cafe S M

14 | 20 | 15 | $17

801 Fourth Ave. (F St.), 619-615-7625
909 Prospect St. (Fay Ave.), La Jolla, 619-456-7625

☑ "Bring the kids – and the earplugs" to these popular chain outlets in La Jolla and the Gaslamp Quarter for a taste of casual American food; they may be "too loud", but they're "reliable" for "rockin' music" and "interesting" memorabilia, though many maintain "we're too old" for this "tourist city."

Harry's Coffee Shop [S] [M] — – – – I

7545 Girard Ave. (bet. Pearl St. & Torrey Pines Rd.), La Jolla, 619-454-7381

"Always packed and always good", this "friendly" "La Jolla institution" is "unbeatable" for "classic" breakfasts of pancakes or eggs Florentine and also offers "Californian dishes with a healthy" bent; it may be a "dive", but it's one of the "best coffee shops in town."

Healthy Chinese Restaurant [S] — – – – I

(fka House of Chinese Gourmet)

4957 Diane Ave. (Clairemont Mesa Blvd.), 619-279-2520

6875 La Jolla Blvd. (Nautilus St.), La Jolla, 619-459-4188 [M]

This recently remodeled Clairemont "community favorite" and its La Jolla sibling are noted for health-oriented Chinese, including the "best won ton soup", low-fat Szechuan dishes and steamed vegetables; the cheerful staff caters to a loyal clientele grown fond of the prices and the low-key surroundings.

Hernandez Hideaway [S] — 17 15 16 $17

19320 Lake Dr. (Rancho Dr.), Escondido, 760-746-1444

■ "They aren't kidding about the 'hideaway'" description at this "secluded", "basic Tex-Mex" in the rural Del Dios area of Escondido, a "secret place for good food" (albeit "not for dieters") and the "best margaritas"; it's "fun to go and experience" the "friendly atmosphere", which is a major plus, since "there's nothing else for miles."

Hershel's Restaurant & Delicatessen [S] [M] — – – – I

1486 Encinitas Blvd. (1 block east of El Camino Real), Encinitas, 760-942-9655

Bring a big appetite to this bustling, vaguely NY-style deli in Encinitas, where the pastrami sandwiches tower above the plates and a slice of cake just might feed a family of four; a pleasant staff keeps things under control.

Hind Quarter [S] [M] — ▽ 17 9 15 $17

7040 Miramar Rd. (bet. Distribution & Production Aves.), 619-566-4292

◪ This Miramar sibling of South Bay's popular Cafe La Maze offers "good beef" and Traditional American seafood that's "well-prepared but ordinary" and "okay for lunch" when "in the area"; despite the value, critics reckon it's just "another beef house."

Hob Nob Hill [S] [M] — 19 14 21 $15

2271 First Ave. (Juniper St.), 619-239-8176

■ Home of "real American food" that "never changes", this "longtime" Downtown favorite serves "the breakfast of champions" to a mixed clientele of yups who "go for power breakfasts" and seniors who savor the "good value"; it may be "old-fashioned", but it bustles at all hours.

Hodad's 🅢🅜

5010 Newport Ave. (Bacon St.), Ocean Beach, 619-224-4623
■ "Hey, dude! the best cheeseburgers in town" ("great, fat, greasy, really messy burgers") are offered at this "funky" Ocean Beach hangout; surfers awaiting the next wave provide the service for a lively, low-budget beach crowd.

HomeTown Buffet 🅢🅜

Clairemont Village, 3007 Clairemont Dr. (Burgener Blvd.),
619-275-4622
Target Shopping Ctr., 10660 Camino Ruiz (Mira Mesa Blvd.),
619-566-9848
University Sq., 5881 University Ave. (College Ave.), 619-583-7373
Hometown Sq., 651 Palomar St. (bet. Broadway & Trolley
Station), Chula Vista, 619-426-0505
390 W. Main St. (bet. Chambers St. & Magnolia Ave.), El Cajon,
619-441-6477
1135 Highland Ave. (Plaza Blvd.), National City, 619-477-7990
Mission Mktpl., 491 College Blvd. (Mission Ave.),
Oceanside, 760-945-6080
288 Rancheros Dr. (W. San Marcos Blvd.), San Marcos,
760-471-9944
Santee Town Ctr., 265 Town Center Pkwy. (Cuyamaca St.),
Santee, 619-562-1555
☑ "You get what you pay for" acknowledge patrons of these chain-operated buffet feederies located in suburbs around the county; "go in hungry" for a "great variety" of American fare that some say is "school cafeteria"–grade.

Hong Kong ⬤🅢🅜

3871 Fourth Ave. (University Ave.), 619-291-9449
☑ "Good for late-night munchies", this "understated" Chinese in the heart of Hillcrest serves "quality food" ("good spicy eggplant") in simple surroundings to a dressed-down clientele that grows more eclectic (it's a "freak show at 3 AM on Saturdays") as the evening wears on.

Hops Bistro & Brewery 🅢🅜

University Towne Ctr., 4353 La Jolla Village Dr. (Genesee Ave.),
619-587-6677
■ "Happening" microbrewery in the Golden Triangle's University Towne Center, where shoppers, families and sometimes a youthful "brewsky crowd" come for "pub food" ("bean soup and fantastic bread sticks"); it can get "pricey", but the "big dishes" and "great beer" get the job done.

House of Munich 🅢

230 Third Ave. (E St.), Chula Vista, 619-426-5172
■ "One of the better German restaurants" around, this Chula Vista veteran is also one of the only Teutons remaining in SD county; the kitsch trappings (for accordion lovers, the "German music adds to the atmosphere") and friendly service charm a mature crowd, as do the hearty portions of traditional fare.

Hsu's Szechuwan Cuisine [S] [M] ▽ 18 | 15 | 17 | $17
9350 Clairemont Mesa Blvd. (Ruffin Rd.), 619-279-9799
■ For "very authentic food" (notably, a "do-it-yourself Mongolian BBQ"), this Szechuan on a commercial corner of Kearny Mesa "will do" for come-as-you-are dining with swift service and fair prices.

Humphrey's by the Bay [S] [M] 18 | 20 | 19 | $26
Humphrey's Half Moon Inn & Suites, 2241 Shelter Island Dr., 619-224-3577
■ Seemingly "improved since its makeover" and the addition of chef Jim Hill, this long-running Shelter Islander is regaining its luster; the New American "coastal cuisine" (the "macadamia-crusted halibut can't be beat"), along with "great views of yachts galore" and outdoor jazz concerts, make this a "mellow" favorite among hipsters of all ages.

Ichiban [S] [M] ⊄ 20 | 9 | 15 | $10
1449 University Ave. (Normal St.), 619-299-7203
■ "Who cares about decor?" ask fans of this "durable" Uptown Japanese that's admired for its "healthy and tasty" food ("love the grilled yellowtail" and "wonderful noodles"); it's "cheap, fast" and "always packed" with patrons who shrug at an interior resembling a "gutted warehouse."

Ida Bailey's [S] [M] 16 | 20 | 17 | $22
Horton Grand Hotel, 311 Island Ave. (4th Ave.), 619-544-1886
◪ Luring trade to this Traditional American is the "old San Diego decor" and "great jazz bar" of the Gaslamp Quarter's Horton Grand Hotel as well as "Victorian atmosphere" and food that has its advocates ("Sunday brunch to die for"), but is also dismissed by some as merely "ordinary."

Il Fornaio [S] [M] 21 | 23 | 19 | $28
Del Mar Plaza, 1555 Camino del Mar (15th St.), Del Mar, 619-755-8876
◪ "The view makes the food even better" at this "posh" Del Mar Italian known for pricey but "very good food" and "great outdoor dining" in a "romantic" setting that's "perfect for watching sunsets"; chic locals warn that they sometimes "feel rushed" in the usually busy, "really noisy" environment.

Il Forno Italian Bistro & Bar [S] [M] 20 | 19 | 20 | $20
909 Prospect St. (bet. Fay & Girard Aves.), La Jolla, 619-459-5010
■ "Gourmet" pizza, pasta and the "best Bolognese sauce" are mainstays at this La Jolla Northern Italian, which also boasts a jumping, "noisy bar"; the mixed crowd makes it a "busy" indoor/outdoor "street side" scene.

Imperial House [M] 16 | 15 | 19 | $28
505 Kalmia St. (6th Ave.), 619-234-3525
◪ "Return to the '50s" and enjoy "warm service" at this Continental "throwback" next to Balboa Park; however, cynics say that the "old-world atmosphere and food" "need sprucing up", citing a "run-of-the-mill" experience.

Imperial Mandarin ●ⓈⓂ   ▽ 18 | 14 | 18 | $13
3904 Convoy St. (south of Balboa Ave.), 619-292-1222
■ The "weekend dim sum" is a hit at this inexpensive Chinese with a Cantonese accent on Convoy Street, SD's Asian restaurant row; "good prices", competent service and comfortable surroundings draw a repeat, "mostly Asian clientele", so the place hops at prime times.

Ingrid's German Restaurant Ⓢ   20 | 15 | 17 | $14
1520 Garnet Ave. (Ingraham St.), Pacific Beach, 619-270-4250
■ "Neighborhood" stalwart where fans "forget the fat grams and enjoy" because "for a taste of real Germany, this is the place"; offering "large portions", plenty of "German hospitality" and all-around value, it makes for "a refreshing change" of pace in a calorie-counters' world.

Inn at the Park ⓈⓂ   ▽ 16 | 15 | 15 | $20
Park Manor Suites, 3167 Fifth Ave. (Spruce St.), 619-296-0057
■ It's the "clubby atmosphere" that defines this "old-fashioned" Continental–New American on the southern flank of Hillcrest; the menu may be "geared towards the unadventurous", but it suits the well-dressed regulars, many of them after-theater types (actors included) who enjoy the bartender's "heavy cocktails."

Islands Fine Burgers & Drinks ⓈⓂ   15 | 17 | 17 | $13
7637 Balboa Ave. (I-805), 619-569-8866
Carmel Mtn. Plaza, 12224 Carmel Mtn. Rd. (Conference Way), 619-485-8075
La Jolla Village Sq., 3351 Nobel Dr. (Villa La Jolla Dr.), La Jolla, 619-455-9945
240 S. Melrose Dr. (Hacienda Blvd.), Vista, 760-631-1535
■ "Fun with the kids" for a "goof-off meal" of "pretty good burgers" (plus "lots of fries!"), these lively suburban chain outlets are an "undeniable value"; the friendly, young staff and "casual, tropical setting" ("surfer dude paradise") also help attract area slackers.

Italia Mia ⓈⓂ   ▽ 18 | 13 | 17 | $14
Lucky-Target Shopping Ctr., 14771 Pomerado Rd. (bet. Ted Williams Pkwy. & Twin Peaks Rd.), Poway, 619-679-9300
■ They "really try to please" at this "always friendly" "neighborhood" trattoria in Poway serving well-priced Northern Italian pastas and pizzas, along with salads and calzones; it's "not bad for the 'burbs", and the "older crowd" appreciates the accommodating service.

Itri ⓈⓂ   ▽ 20 | 19 | 21 | $24
835 Fourth Ave. (bet. E & F Sts.), 619-234-6538
■ For "authentic Italian cooking in a small, bistro" setting, look no further than this "friendly" Gaslamp "favorite", which features fine service, bright decor and a "good sidewalk" vantage point for scoping the passing multitudes.

Jack & Giulio's [S] [M] | 19 | 15 | 18 | $20 |

2391 San Diego Ave. (bet. Arista St. & Old Town Ave.), 619-294-2074

■ With its "romantic feel", this Italian ("a restaurant in Old Town that's not Mexican!") is a "favorite place" for "moderately priced" specialties like "superb" scampi and chicken cacciatore; not surprisingly, it continues to be "very popular" with longtime followers.

Jake's Del Mar [S] [M] | 19 | 23 | 19 | $26 |

1660 Coast Blvd. (15th St.), Del Mar, 619-755-2002

◪ You "can't beat" the "beautiful ocean view" at this packed ("great place to eat if you can get a seat") New American seafooder on Del Mar beach; its Southern Californian atmosphere makes it a good choice "for business meals or dates", and though dissenters claim "the view is better than the food", the "fabulous" decor and "romantic" room are enough for its admirers.

Jared's [S] | – | – | – | E |

880 E. Harbor Island Dr. (east end of Harbor Island), 619-291-1028

"Be very hungry" when you hit this "great American meat show" for the expense-account set; the steaks and seafood are "consistently" well-executed and the "quaint dining room" – on a stern-wheeler moored at the tip of Shelter Island – is one of a kind; professional service and an "awesome view" keep the clientele more than content.

Jasmine [S] [M] | 23 | 15 | 17 | $20 |

4609 Convoy St. (Baggett St.), 619-268-0888

◪ The "dim sum is wonderful" at this "bustling" Chinese that's celebrated for "authentic" fare that some consider the best "this side of Hong Kong"; the "fine, fresh" seafood is a standout, but, predictably, the place's popularity leads to a "loud" atmosphere and "long waits."

Jimmy Carter's Cafe [S] [M] | 18 | 14 | 18 | $13 |

3172 Fifth Ave. (Spruce St.), 619-295-2070

■ For "unusual" "coffee shop food without the counter", Hillcrest regulars gather at this "little diner"; the "usually pleasant" service and "nice owner", Jimmy Carter (nope, no relation), contribute to a "delightful" experience in the eyes of the laid-back crowd.

Jin Sang [M] | – | – | – | E |

7614 Fay Ave. (bet. Kline & Pearl Sts.), La Jolla, 619-456-4545

At this "lovely" La Jolla Japanese yearling, shabu-shabu – a one-pot meal of beef, chicken or seafood, simmered in a subtle broth with vegetables and noodles – is the star of the show; while other "traditional" dishes are "authentic" and "beautifully presented", some find the flavors "too bland."

Joe's Crab Shack [S][M] — | — | — | M

Hazard Ctr., 7610 Hazard Ctr. Dr. (Friars Rd. E.), Mission Valley, 619-260-1111

While this over-decorated Mission Valley branch of a national seafood chain looks like Mardi Gras gone awry, the genial servers, loud music and nonstop revelry draw a casual, young crowd and a surprising number of families for fun, games and a menu based on crab and other seafood.

Johnny Rockets [S][M] 17 | 19 | 16 | $11

Del Mar Plaza, 1555 Camino del Mar (15th St.), Del Mar, 619-755-1954

■ "Feel like a teenager" again at this cheap "'50s-style diner" with a "classic malt shop look" and a "simple menu" that "kids love", 'cause "for a burger, it's unbeatable"; the location in hip Del Mar Plaza and the "lively" setting make for a "rockin' great" time for the "young" and the "retro" alike.

John's Waffle Shop [S][M]≠ 17 | 9 | 16 | $10

7906 Girard Ave. (Wall St.), La Jolla, 619-454-7371

◪ A La Jolla "village landmark" with a "small-town feel", this "hole-in-the-wall" remains a haven for inexpensive, "old-fashioned breakfasts", with "fun and tasty" choices like the "wonderful chocolate chip pancakes" and "worth-the-wait" waffles; however, foes feel it's "gone downhill" and could use some spiffing up.

Jose's Courtroom [S][M] 16 | 13 | 18 | $14

1037 Prospect St. (bet. Girard & Herschel Aves.), La Jolla, 619-454-7655

■ This "low-rent Mexican smack-dab in the heart of hoity-toity La Jolla" has a rep for "good chips and margaritas" and "consistent, non-challenging food"; more than just a "fun, late-night spot", it's a "rite of passage" for the university students and beach types who show up for the "action" and keep it "noisy."

Juke Joint Cafe [S] ▽ 21 | 22 | 19 | $21

327 Fourth Ave. (bet. J & K Sts.), 619-232-7685

◪ "Wonderful Soul Food" makes this high-stepping Gaslamp Quarter newcomer an "excellent addition to SD" and thanks to the "great jazz" (live Thursday–Sunday), its devotees "love to make it a night there"; a few consider it "kinda pricey" for the experience, but the "interesting food" and ambiance attract the younger, cooler types.

Jyoti-Bihanga [M] ▽ 23 | 18 | 18 | $13

3351 Adams Ave. (Felton St.), 619-282-4116

■ Aging hippies and youthful vegans gather for a "serene dining experience" at this "off-the-beaten-path" "Vegetarian pearl" in up-and-coming University Heights; the "tasty health food in clean surroundings" can be "amazing" ("great faux meat loaf") and the "unhurried atmosphere", "good prices" and pleasant "vibes" also win kudos.

Kabul West Ⓜ🚭
∇ 20 | 14 | 19 | $15
9450 Scranton Rd. (Mira Mesa Blvd.), 619-224-8200
■ "The owners personally prepare and serve" "good ethnic food" spiked with "wonderful spices" at this popular Afghan that recently relocated to Mira Mesa; a decor inspired by native motifs and easygoing prices add to its appeal.

Kaiserhof Ⓢ
21 | 17 | 18 | $22
2253 Sunset Cliffs Blvd. (W. Point Loma Blvd.), Ocean Beach, 619-224-0606
☑ "Classic Teutonic fare and hospitality" make this "cute place" in Ocean Beach "the best German in town", with "authentic", if "heavy", dishes (it's "the only place for Christmas goose" and "great sausages" too); there's also a wide selection of German beers and wines.

Kansas City Barbeque ●ⓈⓂ
16 | 13 | 15 | $14
610 W. Market St (bet. Harbor Dr. & Kettner Blvd.), 619-231-9680
☑ "Tom Cruise fans" know that the "tacky" bar scene in *Top Gun* was filmed at this "pretty good BBQ shack" Downtown that "takes you back to simpler times" with "delicious", "old-fashioned ribs" and "friendly service"; but critics, citing "disappointing, greasy food" say it's "more for nostalgia than anything else."

Karen Krasne's Extraordinary Desserts ⓈⓂ
28 | 20 | 16 | $11
2929 Fifth Ave. (bet. Palm & Quince Sts.), 619-294-7001
■ Sweet news for sybarites: this Hillcrest bakery/cafe with a "lovely setting" that includes a garden would be the top-ranked establishment in SD if it were a full-service eatery, but it has "no competition" in its own class for "haute" desserts; a visit is a "decadent" way to finish an evening, despite some gripes about "long lines" and "off-puttingly curt" service.

Karinya ⓈⓂ
21 | 16 | 18 | $20
825 Garnet Ave. (Mission Blvd.), Pacific Beach, 619-270-5050
■ "Long-running and reliable", this "wonderfully spicy Thai" "favorite" in Pacific Beach is "a hidden gem" with an "extensive menu" of "perfectly seasoned" fare ("love the fiery Cornish hen"); while the ambiance is "low-key", a few complain about an "indifferent", "annoyingly slow" staff.

Karl Strauss Brewery & Grill ⓈⓂ
18 | 18 | 18 | $18
1157 Columbia St. (B St.), 619-234-2739
1044 Wall St. (Herschel Ave.), La Jolla, 619-551-2739
■ "Like sausage" or "great beer, burgers and onion rings?", then come to "San Diego's original brewpub" Downtown (or its younger sibling in La Jolla), where a simple American menu (with some "good German dishes" too), "friendly service" and lively crowd make it a "fun" "favorite" at night, as well as a "popular lunch venue for professionals"; N.B. brewery tours are available.

Karl Strauss Brewery Gardens [S][M] 18 | 23 | 18 | $18
9675 Scranton Rd. (Mira Mesa Blvd.), 619-587-2739
■ "I'll take my beer with a little Zen", please, in the "beautiful, peaceful Japanese garden setting" – a "hidden paradise" – at this American brewery/restaurant in Sorrento Mesa; despite "ordinary bar food", a "terrific" staff that "aims to please" makes it a "good standby for a business lunch" and it's also "pleasant for brunch"; a few find that the "great [live] jazz" and contemporary music make it "way too noisy at night."

Katzra [M] ▽ 21 | 12 | 16 | $15
4229 Convoy St. (Balboa Ave.), 619-279-3430
■ Set on Convoy Street's Asian restaurant row, this "casual place" is "fun for a celebration", thanks to the "hilarious sushi chefs" who preside over the "great bar"; the "good, inexpensive Japanese" fare attracts a clientele that's more interested in quality and value than decor (or lack thereof).

Kazumi Sushi [S] ▽ 21 | 16 | 18 | $20
3965 Fifth Ave. (bet. University Ave. & Washington St.), 619-682-4054
■ "I love Kazumi!" enthuse hip, Uptown fans who applaud the "fantastic sushi" and "superb nambeyaki soup" at this stylish Japanese in the heart of Hillcrest; located near an art cinema, it's "convenient" for dining "before the theater", and the "great host", "accommodating servers" and cheerful mood make it a popular choice.

KC's Tandoor [M] 21 | 8 | 14 | $11
Friars Mission Ctr. Mall, 5608 Mission Ctr. Rd. (Frazee Rd.), 619-497-0751 [S]
Sorrento Food Ct., 9450 Scranton Rd. (north of Mira Mesa Blvd.), 619-535-1941
■ "Indian fast food at its best" can be found at these "informal", if "no-atmosphere", take-out and buffet eateries in Mission Valley and Sorrento Mesa shopping center food courts; the "knowledgeable staff" delivers "tasty", "freshly made" fare – "superb curries", "wonderful tandoori chicken" and "great naan" – at "really good-value" prices.

KEMO SABE [S][M] 22 | 23 | 21 | $27
3958 Fifth Ave. (bet. University Ave. & Washington St.), 619-220-6802
■ "Wild taste combinations that shake up the palate" make "outstanding" chef Deborah Scott "my idol" raves the "tony crowd" that patronizes this top-ranked "spicy" Southwesterner in Hillcrest; the "innovative" cuisine, sparked with Native American and Asian accents, is "distinctive", "exceptionally delicious" (the signature "skirts on fire" steak dish is "superb") and "spectacularly presented" in a "stunning" room by an "attentive" staff; while the "noise level is overwhelming", "everything else is so good, you don't care much."

Kenny's Steak Pub Ⓜ   19 | 21 | 18 | $26
939 Fourth Ave. (Broadway), 619-231-8500
◪ "They try hard" at this "under-appreciated business lunch" spot and steakhouse in Gaslamp (look for the John Wayne statue outside), where the "great filet mignon" offers "good value for the money"; critical carnivores, however, think the "ordinary steaks" are "too expensive for what's offered" and the service can be "disappointing."

Kensington Grill Ⓢ Ⓜ   21 | 19 | 20 | $25
4055 Adams Ave. (bet. Kensington & Terrace Drs.), 619-281-4014
▧ At this "chummy neighborhood joint with clever cooking", the kitchen takes an "imaginative approach" to New American cuisine and regulars say that "everything on the menu is delicious"; an "intimate", "antique-filled" "oasis" with a "quiet atmosphere", it offers "cool vibes", along with perhaps the city's largest list of wines by the glass, to a young, "interesting crowd" drawn from the smart Kensington area; service, however, can be "pleasant" or "uncaring", depending upon the draw.

Khatoon Persian Cuisine Ⓢ Ⓜ ▽ 18 | 14 | 16 | $17
639 Pearl St. (Draper Ave.), La Jolla, 619-459-4016
▧ In a "homelike atmosphere" with pleasant ethnic decor, this small Persian in La Jolla features "filling and tasty" traditional dishes that may "not be too creative", but it's "handy before the movies" and prices are moderate.

Khyber Pass Afghan Ⓢ Ⓜ   21 | 19 | 20 | $18
Empire Sq., 4647 Convoy St. (north of Balboa Ave.), 619-571-3749
▧ With a "unique" "cave-like decor, *Flintstones*-style", and a "great Middle Eastern buffet", this "exotic" Afghan makes for an "interesting" "change of pace" in the East Asian–dominated Convoy Street district; from the "terrific" menu, sample the "unusual" vegetarian plates served by an "excellent" staff in a "fun atmosphere."

Kiyo's Japanese Restaurant Ⓜ   – | – | – | M
531 F St. (bet. 5th & 6th Aves.), 619-238-1726
"Friendly chef Kiyo" is a "witty presence behind the counter" of "our favorite sushi bar" (the oldest in SD and recently remodeled), a low-key Gaslamp Quarter hideaway with "fresh" raw fish and cooked Japanese dishes like "the best tempura"; "it's small, so don't tell too many people."

Kobe Misono Ⓢ   21 | 19 | 20 | $23
5451 Kearny Villa Rd. (Clairemont Mesa Blvd.), 619-560-7399
◪ The entertaining chefs put on a "good show" with their "choreographed cooking" at the teppan tables of this long-running Japanese in Kearny Mesa, where the "teriyaki is the best around" (for those afraid of knives, "good sushi" is available); however, cons complain about "sharing a table with strangers and eating food piecemeal."

Kono's Cafe [S][M]🚫 — 23 | 19 | 22 | $8
704 Garnet Ave. (west of Mission Blvd.), Pacific Beach, 619-483-1669
■ There's "nothing finer than a Sunday morning here" at this Pacific Beach "bargain", voted the top Traditional American in SD; "bring the family dog and sit outside" on the patio and enjoy the "awesome ocean view" while digging into "huge portions" of such "dynamite" fare as "unsurpassed breakfast burritos", "pancakes that taste like mom whipped them up", "delicious, fluffy eggs and cheesy potatoes"; "lines are long", but "service is quick" and it's "always worth the wait."

Korea House [S][M] — 21 | 15 | 17 | $17
4620 Convoy St. (north of Balboa Ave.), 619-560-0080
■ "You'll have fun just trying to figure out the different varieties of kimchi" at this "authentic, flavorful" Korean on restaurant-rich Convoy Street, which serves "a lot of food for the dollar" to an experienced crowd that thinks it's "great fun cooking" the "yummy barbecue" on the grill "at your table"; a disgruntled few, though, grumble "if I'm going to cook my own food, I might as well stay home."

Korean Seoul House [M] — ▽ 22 | 16 | 18 | $16
2121 Adams Ave. (Mississippi St.), 619-299-3571
■ "Really great Korean barbecue" is the attraction at this small Normal Heights standby brightened with native artwork; even if "the menu is limited, everything on it is just right" – "hot, spicy" and "tasty."

LA BONNE BOUFFE [S] — 24 | 17 | 21 | $31
Town & Country Shopping Ctr., 471 Encinitas Blvd. (bet. El Camino Real & I-5), Encinitas, 760-436-3081
■ Slightly "out of the way", "tucked in a shopping strip" in Encinitas, this "quaint", "old-world" "gem" is "a find" for "old-fashioned, Country French" cuisine that admirers swoon reaches "the height of taste sensations" ("wonderful duck and onion soup"), even though the "menu and specials never seem to change"; the chef-owner is "charming" and the service is "personable" but "uneven", sometimes resulting in "long waits for food" that's so "delicious" that some complain of "too-small portions."

La Bruschetta [S][M] — 18 | 17 | 18 | $25
2151 Avenida de la Playa (La Jolla Shores Dr.), La Jolla, 619-551-1221
◪ "Accommodating chef" Nino Zizzo is "really trying hard" to make this Italian in La Jolla Shores *che buono,* turning out "food that smacks of authenticity" ("excellent pastas" and osso buco) amid a "pleasant ambiance" that reminds the prosperous clientele of "a neighborhood trattoria in Italy"; detractors, however, gripe that it "lacks pizazz."

Lader's of La Mesa ⓢ   ▽ 16 | 12 | 14 | $24 |
*Vons Plaza, 5654 Lake Murray Blvd. (Baltimore Dr.), La Mesa,
619-463-9919*
☑ Partisans of the Italian "home cooking" at this "casual
neighborhood" trattoria say it "stands out in La Mesa", and
while 'gourmet' it ain't, the food is "rich"; critics warn of
tabs that seems "expensive for the atmosphere."

Lael's ⓢ Ⓜ   22 | 19 | 20 | $28 |
*Hyatt Regency Hotel, 1 Market Pl. (Seaport Village),
619-232-1234*
■ The "delightful buffets" (particularly Thursday's standout
prime rib feast) offer "great" food and "lots of it" in the main
room at Downtown's ritzy Hyatt Regency; the regular menu
"can be very good" and the setting is "relaxed", too – "not
bad for a hotel dining room."

La Especial Norte, Too ⓢ Ⓜ   ▽ 18 | 9 | 14 | $12 |
*664 N. Coast Hwy. 101 (bet. Encinitas & Leucadia Blvds.),
Encinitas, 760-942-1040*
■ A lively surfer crew likes the taste of "authentic Mexico"
just "fine" at this Encinitas institution and in the absence
of decor, concentrates on "awesome" tortilla and posole
soups, two highlights on a "varied", inexpensive menu.

La Fonda ⓢ Ⓜ   24 | 17 | 19 | $21 |
5752 La Jolla Blvd. (Bird Rock Ave.), La Jolla, 619-456-7171
■ Given that it's the offspring of a respected Tijuana
restaurante, it's no surprise that the "excellent flavors" at
this "upscale" spot in the Bird Rock section of La Jolla
make it the top Mexican in town; it's the place to sample
"unusual" "regional dishes" that are "fun to explore", but
allow plenty of time – the service "needs to speed up."

La Gran Tapa ⓢ Ⓜ   19 | 18 | 19 | $21 |
611 B St. (6th Ave.), 619-234-8272
■ Modeled after a noted Madrid tapas bar, this "clubby
urban oasis" Downtown serves "true Spanish" cuisine,
offering a "different and authentic" experience; the
"cosmopolitan" ambiance adds to the appeal.

La Jolla Brewing Co. ⓢ Ⓜ   16 | 16 | 16 | $15 |
7536 Fay Ave. (Pearl St.), La Jolla, 619-456-2739
☑ "Fresh brews" are the main attraction for a younger
crowd that revels in the "relaxed" atmosphere of this
Californian microbrewery; while the "unspectacular", "bar-
type" eats are beside the point, a "good burger and beer"
meet most expectations here.

La Mesa Ocean Grille ⓢ Ⓜ   – | – | – | M |
5465 Lake Murray Blvd. (Maryland Ave.), La Mesa, 619-463-1548
Neighborhood residents drop by this East County seafooder
for informal meals of chowder and tasty, simple fare; it
may be decor-resistant and low on ambiance, but it has
the virtues of convenience and pleasant service.

Lamont Street Grill ⓢⓂ   21 | 21 | 21 | $26
4445 Lamont St. (bet. Garnet & Grand Aves.), Pacific Beach,
619-270-3060

☑ A fireplace-lit patio is a "cozy" feature at this "old-time
fave" for Californian "fine dining" that's set in a remodeled
Pacific Beach house; it's a "charming" and "romantic"
"place to get engaged", though some sense "a menu
update" may be overdue.

La Paloma   – | – | – | M
Restaurant & Cantina ⓢⓂ
116 Escondido Ave. (E. Vista Way), Vista, 760-758-7140
Some regard the "innovative" food at this "unusually good"
Vista cantina on a par with that of the "best gourmet
Mexicans in San Diego"; a "low-key ambiance, charming
surroundings and great service" also keep it a local favorite.

La Provence ⓢⓂ   18 | 21 | 15 | $26
708 Fourth Ave. (G St.), 619-544-0661

☑ "The look and mood" are pure Provençal, drawing
Francophiles to this "charming" Gaslamp bistro; though
the "delightful" decor shines and the "enjoyable" cooking
tries to live up to it, foes warn the results are as "uneven" as
the service; N.B. due to a change in ownership, menu and
staff, the above food and service ratings are now outdated.

La Salsa ⓢⓂ   20 | 11 | 15 | $9
Costa Verde Ctr., 8750 Genesee Ave. (La Jolla Village Dr.),
619-455-7229
San Diego Int'l Airport, west terminal, 3707 N. Harbor Dr.,
619-296-3789
415 Horton Plaza (4th Ave.), 619-234-6906
Black Mtn. Village, 9172 Mira Mesa Blvd. (Black Mtn. Rd.),
619-530-0607
1010 University Ave. (10th Ave.), 619-543-0778
Coronado Plaza Shopping Ctr., 1360 Orange Ave. (R.H.
Dana), Coronado, 619-435-7778
219 N. El Camino Real (Encinitas Blvd.), Encinitas, 760-436-9266
1290 Auto Pkwy. (Valley Pkwy.), Escondido, 760-739-9817
North County Fair Mall, 200 E. Via Rancho Pkwy. (I-15),
Escondido, 760-747-6605
4990 Baltimore Dr. (El Cajon Blvd.), La Mesa, 619-589-6696
980 Grand Ave. (Cass St.), Pacific Beach, 619-483-1007

■ This countywide Mexican chain offers "consistently good
and fresh" fast food in a "clever Mexican atmosphere";
it's big with fans of "bargain prices", especially those who
say olé to "healthy", "low-fat" eating.

La Scala ⓢⓂ   ∇ 21 | 17 | 19 | $20
1101 Scott St. (Canon St.), Point Loma, 619-224-2272

■ Located near Shelter Island, this is a "neighborhood
favorite" for a Point Loma crowd that shows up for a
traditional taste of Southern Italy; the "great" staff and
"homey" ambiance help secure its status as an "old reliable."

Las Olas 🅂🅼
20 | 16 | 17 | $13

2655 S. Coast Hwy. 101 (Manchester Ave.),
Cardiff-by-the-Sea, 760-942-1860

◪ When the urge arises for an "outstanding fish taco platter", this "funky" Mexican awaits in Cardiff-by-the-Sea; the faithful "love this place" for the "nice location", servers who "try so hard" and cheap prices, but doubters shrug at "just ok" eats.

La Taverna 🅼
– | – | – | M

927 Silverado St. (Girard Ave.), La Jolla, 619-454-0100

This La Jolla Italian, now run by the Vitale family, is so tiny that the crowd spills right out onto the sidewalk terrace; Mama is the "stellar chef" and her sons serve her irresistible homemade sausages and linguine with gorgonzola sauce; those already smitten advise "keep an eye on this one."

La Terrazza 🅂🅼
▽ 22 | 19 | 20 | $23

8008 Girard Ave. (Prospect St.), La Jolla, 619-459-9750

■ Set in a "lovely location near La Jolla Cove", this Italian is "still somewhat undiscovered", but given its "excellent cuisine" and the "sophisticated" decor that dresses up the "beautiful room" with a view, that could change; it's already a fave for La Jollans and visitors in designer sportswear.

LAUREL RESTAURANT & BAR 🅂🅼
26 | 26 | 22 | $38

505 Laurel St. (5th Ave.), 619-239-2222

◪ "The place to take guests who think SD is a hick town" say admirers of this "sleek, sexy", dinner-only New French near Balboa Park, with a "big-city feel" that gives an extra edge to Douglas Organ's "superb" cuisine; as you'd expect from the younger sister of WineSellar & Brasserie, there's an "excellent wine list"; so even if some find it noisy, with uneven service, more "wish they were open for lunch."

La Vache & Co. 🅂🅼
19 | 16 | 18 | $23

420 Robinson Ave. (4th Ave.), 619-295-0214

◪ The "pommes frites rule" at this "cozy" Country French, a "great addition to Hillcrest" where the "stylish" fare entices an eclectic crowd; a few skeptics are "not impressed", though, dismissing it as "pedestrian."

La Valencia 🅂🅼
23 | 25 | 23 | $36

La Valencia Hotel, 1132 Prospect St. (Herschel Ave.), La Jolla, 619-454-0771

■ For its prosperous, "old-time" clientele, the three major rooms at "La Jolla's pink palace" remain the places to see, be seen and enjoy both power dining and "romantic" interludes in French, Continental and American style; this is "elegant California" with "gracious" service in "luxurious" surroundings, where the "Sky Room has a fabulous view and great food", the Whaling Bar is a "classic" and the "lovely" Mediterranean Room is "great" for brunch on the patio.

Le Bambou 🅂
20 | 16 | 19 | $21

2634 Del Mar Heights Rd. (Mango Dr.), Del Mar, 619-259-8138

■ A "neighborhood favorite", this "authentic Vietnamese" is a "Del Mar hideaway" that's "worth the trip"; the "yummy" cuisine ("clay-pot everything") and "pleasant service" make the "simple setting" attractive to a casually chic crowd that can live with the "small portions."

LE FONTAINEBLEAU 🅂🅼
22 | 26 | 24 | $41

Westgate Hotel, 1055 Second Ave. (Broadway), 619-557-3655

☑ There's been a dramatic shift in direction for this gorgeous but staid dowager among Downtown restaurants; after years of serving subpar cuisine in one of the most tastefully appointed hotel dining rooms in Cal, management has installed chef Rene Herbeck (ex Marius) in the kitchen and the results should be impressive – welcome news for those who like their French cuisine hot and haute; N.B. the food rating does not reflect this chef change.

L'Escale 🅂🅼
∇ 21 | 22 | 20 | $33

Coronado Island Marriott Resort, 2000 Second St. (Glorietta Bay Blvd.), Coronado, 619-435-3000

☑ "What's cooking?" ask those who say the New American food at this hotel dining room, though "reliable", is "not as special" since the property became the Coronado Island Marriott; still, this "pretty restaurant" with a "soothing atmosphere" continues to offer a "great" bay view and "pleasant outdoor dining in the summertime."

Liaison 🅂
19 | 16 | 19 | $31

2202 Fourth Ave. (Ivy St.), 619-234-5540

☑ "Win big points with the wife or girlfriend" at this Classic French near Balboa Park, where the Gallic specialties, "charming" service and "rustic" setting remind nostalgists of their "first trip to Paris"; though a few find it "pretty average", pros say that the "prix fixe menu is a great buy."

Little Russia 🅂🅼
∇ 11 | 8 | 10 | $22

6130 Lake Murray Blvd. (El Paso St.), La Mesa, 619-465-7070

■ Live entertainment isn't enough to placate those who have found this La Mesa Russian "a pitiful place" that offers "skimpy servings" of "second-rate" fare; when the music plays on weekends "be ready to join the party", which is dominated by Russian émigrés who seem to ignore the cooking in favor of noisy fellowship.

Little Tokyo 🅂🅼
17 | 13 | 17 | $13

Carmel Mtn. Plaza, 11640 Carmel Mtn. Rd. (Rancho Carmel Dr.), 619-675-1468

■ "Udon soup to die for on a cold evening" is a drawing card at this "good deal" of a Japanese in Carmel Mountain Plaza mall; the "original" approach of offering noodles and sushi on the fly makes it an option "for fast Japanese" when convenience matters more than technique.

Living Room Coffeehouse [S][M] 18 | 18 | 15 | $9

5900 El Cajon Blvd. (59th St.), 619-286-8434 ◐
1417 University Ave. (Richmond St.), 619-295-7911 ◐
1010 Prospect St. (Girard Ave.), La Jolla, 619-459-1187

■ These "hangouts" in La Jolla, Hillcrest and the SDSU district are so "warm, comfy and unique" that the young college clientele is happy "to settle in for a while" and "meet friends here when the house is too dirty"; the cheap, light fare, "good desserts" and "great coffee" compensate for the "no table service" policy.

Lobster Co. [M] ▽ 18 | 22 | 21 | $28

420 E. St. (bet. 4th & 5th Aves.), 619-233-3377

■ The "whimsical" undersea theme at this "big, new lobster house in Gaslamp" recalls "Disneyland's submarine ride", a "clever idea whose time may have come"; noted chef Christian Vignes offers a traditional seafood menu starring lobster, which is "good", if a tad "expensive", but the conventioneer trade may create an atmosphere that's "too casual" for the bucks.

Longhorn Cafe [S][M] ▽ 20 | 14 | 17 | $12

Mission Gorge Shopping Ctr., 6519 Mission Gorge Rd. (bet. Friars Rd. & Zion Ave.), 619-283-0831

■ "We go before baseball games" say regulars at this comfortable, if slightly "ratty", bar-cum-eatery near the stadium in Mission Gorge; a Traditional American menu featuring "fabulous hamburgers" is served in a setting that revolves around the "John Wayne room" (a "must see"), and many testify that the atmosphere "always makes me want to have a long-neck beer."

Lorna's Italian Kitchen [S][M] 21 | 11 | 17 | $15

University Sq. Shopping Ctr., 3945 Governor Dr. (Genesee Ave.), 619-452-0661

◩ It may be a "hole-in-the-wall", but the "real homemade" Italian food at this University City "local favorite" ensures that the space is usually "noisy" and "crowded", minor inconveniences in the eyes of a clientele that "loves" the "pasta galore" and "good value" – "every neighborhood should have" a place like this.

Lotsa Pasta [S][M] 20 | 15 | 18 | $13

Pacific Plaza, 1762 Garnet Ave. (bet. Jewel & Lamont Sts.), Pacific Beach, 619-581-6777

◩ Offering "choices, choices, choices", this "cheap and good" Italian tucked in the back corner of a Pacific Beach shopping center specializes in "quick and tasty" pastas and sauces that are easy to "mix and match", plus an "incredible" meat pie known as timpano; "casual" and "friendly", the "simple" setting is favored by an informal beach-area crowd that finds it "ideal" "for takeout", though a few quibblers shrug "nothing remarkable."

Machupicchu Peruvian S
— | — | — | M
4755 Voltaire St. (Sunset Cliffs Blvd.), Ocean Beach,
619-222-2656
As the "only Peruvian in town", this ethnic in easygoing
Ocean Beach may have the market for Andean cuisine
cornered, but even laid-back locals wish the decor was
spiffier and the service friendlier.

Maharajah S
— | — | — | I
Uptown District Shopping Ctr., 1220 Cleveland Ave. (bet.
University Ave. & Vermont St.), 619-543-1163
They're serving "above-average Indian" at this spot in
Hillcrest's popular Uptown District, but while the "food is
good", some contend the room has "no style"; in general,
though, the wallet-friendly prices and cheerful service
balance out the "disappointing" decor.

Maitre D'
24 | 23 | 24 | $41
5523 La Jolla Blvd. (bet. Forward & Midway Sts.), La Jolla,
619-456-2111
■ When "money's no object", this "old-fashioned" Classic
French in La Jolla is a "place for special occasions";
owner Louis Zalesjak ("as much a performance artist as a
restaurateur") lays on the "old-world charm" as he "goes
out of his way" to make "an experience" of premium cuisine
and "elegant" surroundings; this is where upscale diners
go when it's time to get "intimate and romantic."

Mandarin China S M
▽ 19 | 16 | 16 | $17
4110 W. Point Loma Blvd. (bet. Midway Dr. & Sports Arena
Blvd.), 619-222-6688
■ Long-running Chinese in the Sports Arena district where
the "wonderful dim sum" is favored by the budget-conscious;
efficient service and a quiet atmosphere are other pluses.

Mandarin Dynasty S M
▽ 18 | 15 | 20 | $17
1458 University Ave. (Normal St.), 619-298-8899
■ This plainly appointed "neighborhood Chinese in Hillcrest"
is praised as a "real find" for specialties like "great sizzling
rice soup"; it's also championed for offering vegetarian
fare to health-conscious chopstick wielders who just
don't do fried pork.

Mandarin Garden S M
▽ 20 | 16 | 15 | $14
Mira Mesa Mall, 8242 Mira Mesa Blvd. (Camino Ruiz),
619-566-4720
■ Discover "Chinese food the way the Chinese like it" at
this "out-of-the-way", somewhat garish Mandarin-style
installment in the Mira Mesa Mall; the chow is so "yummy"
that the "smells will drag you in the door", which along with
reasonable prices accounts for its bustling atmosphere.

Mandarin House [S][M] 19 | 15 | 18 | $17

2604 Fifth Ave. (Maple St.), 619-232-1101
6765 La Jolla Blvd. (Bonair St.), La Jolla, 619-454-2555
◩ These venerable Downtown and La Jolla Chinese serve "popular" dishes "geared to American" tastes, along with "some authentic specialties"; while some say this duo has "passed its prime", their quiet ambiance and seasoned service have earned them "sentimental favorite" status.

Manhattan [S][M] – | – | – | E

Empress Hotel, 7766 Fay Ave. (Silverado St.), La Jolla, 619-459-0700
Evocative of a "retro" "New York–style restaurant", this "charming" Italian in La Jolla's Empress Hotel impresses with an "excellent" menu ("fabulous lamb recipes", the "greatest veal chop on earth") and "many tableside preparations"; some of the "best waiters in town" work the "romantic" room "attentively", though a few think the decor "needs a face-lift."

Maranto's Mardi Gras Cafe [S][M] – | – | – | I

3185 Midway Dr. (bet. East Dr. & Rosecrans St.), 619-223-5501
Tucked away in a nondescript strip mall in the Midway District, this tiny Cajun-Creole treasure manages to squeeze in a few tables among shelves groaning with Louisiana canned goods, cookbooks and hot sauces of every stripe; expect grand New Orleans gumbos, jambalayas and muffalettas – high-rise sandwiches of Italian cold cuts, cheese and olive salad, layered on crusty, round loaves.

MARINE ROOM [S][M] 23 | 26 | 22 | $37

2000 Spindrift Dr. (Torrey Pines Rd.), La Jolla, 619-459-7222
■ "Right on the ocean (and sometimes in it)", this "elegant" French on the surf in La Jolla is "unsurpassed" for its "famous view", and with chef Bernard Guillas working "wonders with the food", there's "new life" in the kitchen; well-dressed "out-of-towners" and local "beautiful people" enjoy the "rich and rewarding" "special-occasion" atmosphere, which combined with the excellent, if "stuffy", service, makes it "always an experience – especially for your wallet."

Market Cafe [S][M] – | – | – | M

Loews Coronado Bay Resort, 4000 Coronado Bay Rd. (Silver Strand Blvd.), Coronado, 619-424-4444
Deemed "cute for a casual meal" and "one of the best" for Sunday brunch, this bright New American at Loews Coronado Bay Resort offers a cheaper "alternative to the costly dining room" (i.e. the hotel's elegant Azzura Point); guests and locals like the cheerful ambiance, but warn that "holiday" crowds can create a hectic scene.

Marrakesh [S][M] 17 | 20 | 19 | $24

634 Pearl St. (Draper Ave.), La Jolla, 619-454-2500

■ Fans of the arts say the "belly dancing's a treat" at this La Jolla "Moroccan experience" where the "exotic" dishes (*b'steeya*, "great couscous") are an "eat-with-your-fingers" "experience", making for a night out that's "unique in SD"; adventurous patrons are rewarded with pleasant service, "authentic" North African decor and "lots of fun."

Mexican Village Restaurant [S] 15 | 16 | 16 | $17

120 Orange Ave. (1st St.), Coronado, 619-435-1822

◪ "This barn has charm" say admirers of this "lively Mexican" in Coronado, serving "huge portions" of "old-fashioned Tex-Mex", though purists shrug at the cooking ("ok if you're a gringo"); a recent remodeling has spruced up its image, which may not be reflected in the decor score.

Miguel's Cocina [S][M] 20 | 19 | 20 | $17

2912 Shelter Island Dr. (Scott St.), 619-224-2401
1351 Orange Ave. (Adella Ave.), Coronado, 619-437-4237

■ A "courtyard setting with trellised vines" makes a "perfect hideaway" at this popular Coronado Mexican (which has a sibling near Shelter Island); "good food and people" combine to create a "colorful" atmosphere where "pleasant, efficient service" and "reasonable prices" have a lot to do with why it's "sometimes a very crowded" scene.

MILLE FLEURS [S][M] 27 | 27 | 26 | $54

Country Squire Courtyard, 6009 Paseo Delicias (Avenida de Acacias), Rancho Santa Fe, 619-756-3085

◪ Set in a blissfully beautiful Mediterranean-style villa in rural Rancho Santa Fe, this "big-bucks" Contemporary French "for the horsey set" features "wonderful" food served in a "romantic" (a few say "stuffy") setting that "looks like France"; if some find the service "pompous" and the "small portions" "grossly overpriced", a majority considers owner Bertrand Hug's discreet retreat "the ideal special-occasion restaurant."

Milligan's Bar & Grill [S] 19 | 20 | 19 | $30

5786 La Jolla Blvd. (1 block north of Bird Rock Ave.), La Jolla, 619-459-7311

◪ Famed for "the perfect martini", this American steakhouse in La Jolla's Bird Rock district is also "dependable" for "jazz and steaks"; though lipid phobes dismiss it as the "home of high cholesterol", fans like the "comfortable atmosphere."

Milton's Deli [S][M] 16 | 14 | 16 | $17

Flower Hill Mall, 2660 Via de la Valle (I-5), 619-792-2225

◪ "If you miss NY", this Del Mar deli is deemed an "adequate" substitute, dishing up "large servings" of standards like chopped liver; dissenters say the "surfer-guy" service seems to need "adult supervision" and kvetch that there's "no pickles on the table."

Miss China Restaurant [S][M]⇏ ▽ 20 | 13 | 20 | $19

2240 Avenida de la Playa (bet. La Jolla Shores Dr. & Paseo del Ocaso), La Jolla, 619-454-2311

■ This "consistently good" Chinese in La Jolla Shores is a "wee", under-decorated spot whose followers rave about its "healthy" cuisine and convenient takeout, though dining in allows one to enjoy the "family feeling" and "friendly" staff ("Miss Kitty is great"); N.B. BYO.

Mission, The [S][M] 22 | 18 | 17 | $11

3795 Mission Blvd. (San Jose Pl.), 619-488-9060
2801 University Ave. (28th St.), 619-220-8992

■ Connoisseurs of breakfast food ("best pancakes in the world", "great rosemary potatoes") dominate the "eclectic crowd" that frequents these decidedly "hip", coffee shop–style Americans in youthful Mission Beach and up-and-coming North Park; "safe places for vegetarians" as well, they offer an "interesting menu", "neat paintings on the wall" and cheap prices.

Mission Coffee Cup [S][M] ▽ 24 | 17 | 20 | $12

1109 Wall St. (bet. Herschel & Ivanhoe Aves.), La Jolla, 619-454-2819

■ Sorry, it's too late to "keep it secret"; this coffee shop in the heart of La Jolla is a "funky", simply decorated American where locals of every stripe gather for cheap chow that partisans nominate for the "best breakfast around" ("loved it!"); N.B. they plan to begin serving dinner in January '99.

Mission Hills Café [S] 20 | 17 | 18 | $18

808 W. Washington St. (bet. Falcon & Goldfinch Sts.), 619-296-8010

■ What a "deal-o-rama" enthuse supporters of this "casual" "neighborhood restaurant" in sedate Mission Hills, where the "basic American dishes" and "fresh desserts" are recognized as a "bargain" "for what you get"; it draws a mature fan base who say it's "usually a hit."

Mister A's [S][M] 20 | 23 | 22 | $37

Fifth Ave. Financial Ctr., 2550 Fifth Ave., 12th fl. (Laurel St.), 619-239-1377

◪ This "classic", "special-occasion" Continental boasts an "endless view" from atop the Fifth Avenue Financial Centre near Balboa Park, but while the expense account–priced food is "still good", critics complain it's "not up to old standards" and the "red-velvet" decor feels "preserved under glass"; ratings are strong, but so is the sense that "service and scenery carry" this "dinosaur."

MIXX [S][M] 23 | 20 | 21 | $28

3671 Fifth Ave. (Pennsylvania Ave.), 619-299-6499

◪ "Innovative food" 'without boundaries' wins 'em over at this "reasonably priced" Eclectic in "trendy" Hillcrest that's quietly decorated to show off the youngish, "see-and-be-seen" crowd; the only points of contention are service that "could be better" and weekend blues and jazz, which some would nix but others savor; otherwise, it's "one of the best newer restaurants."

Montanas American Grill [S][M] 22 | 20 | 21 | $26

1421 University Ave. (Richmond Ave.), 619-297-0722

■ "Spice and variety" is the rule at this thoroughly "modernistic" bar and grill in Hillcrest that's admired for its "somewhat eclectic" take on American carnivore classics ("good ol' Southern BBQ ribs", "great mixed grill"); a "minimalist" design lends "sophistication" and an animated clientele keeps the room "loud."

MORTON'S OF CHICAGO [S][M] 26 | 24 | 25 | $48

285 J St. (bet. 2nd & 3rd Aves.), 619-696-3369

■ Meat lovers would gladly "take out a second mortgage" to finance a trip to this "dark", "woody", casually elegant Downtown steak palace serving notoriously "huge portions" of the "best beef this side of Chicago"; of course, cost isn't an issue for the expense-account crowd that heads here for "first-class" food and service, and though a few find the raw meat menu cart shtick too much, most admirers aren't cowed by it.

Mr. Sushi [S] 22 | 12 | 19 | $18

1535 Garnet Ave. (Ingraham St.), Pacific Beach, 619-581-2664

■ "If you can get in", "eat at the bar" for the best access to the "wonderful" sushi at this "busy, busy" Japanese in Pacific Beach, where an informal, younger crowd puts up with "spartan" surroundings and "long lines" to sample "delectable" fish at at swallowable prices.

Neiman's [S][M] 17 | 18 | 18 | $21

300 Carlsbad Village Dr. (Hwy. 101), Carlsbad, 760-729-4131

◪ A "relaxing lunch spot" by day, this "basic American" in a historic Victorian mansion in Carlsbad cuts loose after dark with live entertainment, including "wonderful big-band swing dancing" on Fridays; foodwise, it "can be good", though doubters deem it just "passable" and save their compliments for the "special touches" that go into the "interesting" 19th-century surroundings.

Newport Ave. Bar & Grill [S][M] ▽ 18 | 14 | 18 | $16
4935 Newport Ave. (bet. Bacon & Cable Sts.), Ocean Beach, 619-222-0168
■ Even those who "don't own a Harley" should "feel welcome" at this Californian "hangout" in Ocean Beach, where the affordable "beach bar food" (crab legs, fries) provides "good quality" without aiming too high; the party-minded regulars don't mind the functional decor as long as they have that inspiring "view at sunset."

94th Aero Squadron [S][M] 17 | 20 | 18 | $21
8885 Balboa Ave. (bet. Hwy. 163 & I-15), 619-560-6771
◪ "Nostalgia for WWI" prevails at this biplane-themed farmhouse overlooking Montgomery Field where loyalists "bring visitors" and tout the "experience"; though critics call the American menu "nothing special", the "unique" setting makes it a "good business-lunch site."

Noodle House of Otemoyan [M] 21 | 8 | 17 | $11
4646 Convoy St. (Opportunity Rd.), 619-268-9595
■ This "cheap", "authentic" Japanese on the Convoy Street Asian restaurant row is a modest, "little hole-in-the-wall", but admirers of its "simple", "delicious" soba and udon dishes swear you "can't go wrong with noodles" or the "great, big bowls of hot Japanese soup."

Old Ox [S][M] 16 | 14 | 17 | $18
4474 Mission Blvd. (Garnet Ave.), 619-275-3790
◪ A "San Diego staple", this ever-popular American in Pacific Beach serves surf 'n' turf to easygoing locals who also appreciate the "budget" weekend brunches and the outdoor seating; however, a minority labels the cuisine "disappointing" – "this is a bar!"

Old Spaghetti Factory [S][M] 16 | 19 | 16 | $13
275 Fifth Ave. (K St.), 619-233-4323
111 N. Twin Oaks Valley Rd. (Hwy. 78), San Marcos, 760-471-0155
◪ Maybe it's "not quite Italian", but this "fun and cheap" Gaslamp veteran is a "family place" that's undeniably "great for kids", thanks to a pasta-heavy menu; even though it seemingly "seats 1,000", expect "a wait" for "food for the masses"; N.B. there's a newer branch in San Marcos.

Old Town Mexican Cafe [S][M] 20 | 16 | 17 | $15
2489 San Diego Ave. (Conde St.), 619-297-4330
■ "Get lost in Margaritaville" advise aficionados of this Old Town Mexican, a "local hangout for *carnitas*" and an established "tourist mecca" that's "great for big parties"; most find the "traditional and good" cuisine and "authentic" atmosphere convincing enough, and everyone "loves the tortillas" because they're handmade "in the front window."

F	D	S	C

OLD TRIESTE 25 | 15 | 23 | $37

2335 Morena Blvd. (bet. Kane & Lister Sts.), 619-276-1841
■ It's the "classic Northern Italian" cuisine that makes this meeting place for the "old San Diego" elite "still one of the best"; it may cost, but the "quiet, romantic" atmosphere and "top-notch service" (the "owner knows and pampers his customers") smoothly combine with the "sophisticated" food to preserve its reputation as a "grand old dame."

Old Venice [S] [M] – | – | – | M

2910 Canon St. (bet. Rosecrans & Scott Sts.), 619-222-5888
"Quiet and easy" with a "great ambiance", this "reputable, eclectic Italian" near Shelter Island is "popular with locals" who like to "hobnob with the yacht club crowd" either in the "attractive bar", the "beautifully decorated" dining room or on the "delightful patio"; its specialties – "great meat sauce, ravioli, pizzas and salads" – can be "wonderful" and there's live jazz and blues on most nights.

Olé Madrid [S] 19 | 20 | 17 | $21

755 Fifth Ave. (bet. F & G Sts.), 619-557-0146
■ "Noisy but fun", this Gaslamp Quarter Spanish features "appetizers big enough for a whole meal" and "hip decor"; the tapas and "pretty good" menu make it "an authentic experience", and afterwards, patrons can "hang with the Euros" at the nightclub upstairs.

Olive Garden [S] [M] 13 | 14 | 16 | $15

3215 Sports Arena Blvd. (2 blocks west of Rosecrans St.), 619-226-2124
1884 Marron Rd. (Jefferson St.), Carlsbad, 760-434-1016
11555 Carmel Mtn. Rd. (I-15), Carmel Mtn. Ranch, 619-485-9873
Chula Vista Ctr., 585 I St. (Broadway), Chula Vista, 619-498-1717
1107 W. Valley Pkwy. (I-15), Escondido, 760-737-9285
Grossmont Shopping Ctr., 5500 Grossmont Ctr. Dr. (bet. Jackson & Murray Drs.), La Mesa, 619-460-7221
◪ These "predictable" chain outlets offer "quick Italian" dining that's "as ordinary as it gets", but those in pursuit of a "value" meal that's "geared to the American family" "can't go wrong here"; however, critics contend that this is "mass-produced" food that's strictly for the "desperate."

Onami [S] [M] 22 | 14 | 13 | $21

(fka Todai)
240 E. Via Rancho Pkwy. (I-15), Escondido, 760-738-7522
◪ "Considering the price, it's a real find" whisper suburbanite fans of this "great Japanese buffet" near Escondido's North County Fair Mall; "a sushi lover's dream", it presents a "wonderful variety" of "fresh", "high-quality" raw fish at "all-you-can-eat" quantities, which compensates for the understated decor, "rude" service and an atmosphere that, "when this place cranks", can be "hectic."

150 Grand Café Ⓜ
`24` `22` `23` `$28`

150 W. Grand Ave. (bet. Broadway & Maple St.),
Escondido, 760-738-6868

■ The "innovative" and "delicious" cuisine at this handsome New American earns repeated kudos as "one of Escondido's culinary saving graces"; the "charming" and "comfortable dining experience", "great attention to detail" and "excellent service" earn still more praise for this "stylish bistro" from admirers who show up in everything from Levis to Armani.

On the Border Ⓢ Ⓜ
`_` `_` `_` `I`

Park Valley Ctr., 1770 Camino de la Reina (bet. Mission Center Rd. & Stadium Way), 619-209-3700

Many of the "recipes are unique" at this cavernous, cowboy-themed chain feedery in Mission Valley, where the kitchen prepares a menu that mingles "excellent" "Mexican with a California twist" with Tex-Mex standards; wash down the fare with "wonderful margaritas" or shots from the "good variety of tequilas."

Original Pancake House Ⓢ Ⓜ
`_` `_` `_` `I`

3906 Convoy St. (south of Balboa Ave.), 619-565-1740
160 S. Rancho Santa Fe Rd. (Manchester Ave.), Encinitas, 760-943-1939
Lucky-Target Ctr., 14905 Pomerado Rd. (Camino del Norte), Poway, 619-679-0186

Celebrated for flipping "the best sizzling apple pancakes in town", this chainlet is popular for its "informal, wonderful breakfasts" – the only meal served (daily, until 3 PM) – that are delivered in simple, pleasant surroundings by an efficient, smiling staff.

Oscar's Ⓢ Ⓜ
`19` `13` `17` `$12`

12045 Carmel Mtn. Rd. (Highland Ranch Rd.), Carmel Mtn. Ranch, 619-592-0222
Parkway Plaza, 375 Parkway Plaza (bet. Fletcher Pkwy. & Johnson Ave.), El Cajon, 619-440-1400
1505 Encinitas Blvd. (El Camino Real), Encinitas, 760-632-0222
8590 Rio San Diego Dr. (Stadium Way), Mission Valley, 619-295-6200

■ Homegrown quartet offering a "family setting" for "hearty, quick meals" of mostly American fare (and pizza, too); even if the "menu is limited", this is a "place the kids like", and parents take comfort in the "good value" and "fast service."

Osteria Panevino Ⓢ Ⓜ
`23` `19` `18` `$27`

722 Fifth Ave. (G St.), 619-595-7959

■ When undecided, "order at random" from the "authentic" menu at this Northern Italian in the Gaslamp Quarter that's a "favorite" for "extraordinary cuisine" ("awesome mushroom risotto") and "rustic Tuscan decor"; it can be "cramped" and "noisy", and some warn of "uncomfortable chairs", but then again "the food's too good to care!"

Outback Steakhouse S M — 19 | 17 | 18 | $21
4196 Clairemont Mesa Blvd. (Clairemont Dr.), 619-274-6283
722 Jamacha Rd. (Washington Ave.), El Cajon, 619-588-4332
5628 Lake Murray Blvd. (Baltimore Dr.), La Mesa, 619-466-9795
14701 Pomerado Rd. (Ted Williams Pkwy.), Poway, 619-486-1563
▨ These "midpriced steak joint" franchises with Aussie attitude are known for "large portions" of "good beef" with deep-fried "bloomin' onions" on the side; typically "very crowded" (impatient types "regret the no-reservations" policy), they're "family-oriented" outposts "for teenagers with big appetites"; but quibblers query: "my steak – was it from a cow or a kangaroo?"

PACIFICA DEL MAR S M — 24 | 24 | 21 | $31
Del Mar Plaza, 1555 Camino del Mar (15th St.), Del Mar, 619-792-0476
▧ With its "beautiful ocean views and lovely, clever food", this American seafooder with "Asian influences" in chic Del Mar Plaza is a stylish "theme park"; the "almost too trendy" menu strikes enthusiasts as "incredible", and combined with the feng shui–correct setting and "sunsets on the shore", explains why a "happy, upscale crowd" arrives in droves.

Pacific Coast Grill S M — 23 | 21 | 20 | $24
Beachwalk Ctr., 437 S. Hwy. 101 (bet. Lomas Santa Fe Dr. & Via de la Valle), Solana Beach, 619-794-4632
▧ More than just a "great people-watching spot", this "pretty, little" Californian in Solana Beach features a "refreshing", marine-oriented menu ("incredible shrimp dumplings"), "good service" and artsy, "eclectic decor" that emanates "good vibes"; fans rate it "very cool."

Palenque S M — 20 | 15 | 13 | $19
1653 Garnet Ave. (bet. Ingraham & Jewell Sts.), 619-272-7816
▨ The "authentic, gourmet Mexican" served at this pleasant, thatch-roofed Pacific Beacher provides "a break" from generic "border food", and the "regional dishes" are laudably "on the spicy side"; it's a "mom-and-pop place" with a "nice atmosphere", but some frown on the "slow service" – "if the food arrives, it's tasty."

Palomino Euro Bistro S M — – | – | – | M
The Aventine, 8990 University Ctr. Ln. (La Jolla Village Dr.), 619-452-9000
An early favorite thanks to its prime location in the sizzling-hot Golden Triangle, this local link of a Seattle-based chain delivers with a surprisingly successful Mediterranean menu of seafood, meats, pastas and specialty pizzas; the bold, extravagant decor (marble, fine woods, paintings, art glass) and carefully trained servers appeal to a crowd that's casual in a decidedly upscale sort of way.

PAMPLEMOUSSE GRILLE 🅂🅜   27 | 24 | 25 | $43
514 Via de la Valle (Jimmy Durante Blvd.), Solana Beach, 619-792-9090
◼ "Beautiful people" and horse-racing types (in season) jockey for a table at this "noisy", art-filled, understatedly elegant Cal-French near the sea, where former NYer Jeffrey Strauss' "imagination and talent" fuel an "exceptional, exciting" menu that's "always a treat", right down to "the best tarte Tatin in San Diego"; still, some label it "overpriced."

Panda Country 🅂🅜   21 | 18 | 19 | $17
4455 Clairemont Mesa Blvd. (Genesee Ave.), 619-270-3930
4150 Regents Rd. (La Jolla Village Dr.), 619-552-1345
Santee Village Sq., 9643 Mission Gorge Rd. (Cuyamaca St.), Santee, 619-449-7061
◼ Purveyors of "consistently good", multiregional Chinese, this trio offers "nice presentations" of "fresh and tasty" food ("seafood dishes are the best bet") at fair prices; the Golden Triangle location is favored for its more elegant digs.

Panda Inn 🅂🅜   22 | 19 | 20 | $19
Horton Plaza Shopping Ctr., 506 Horton Plaza (4th Ave.), 619-233-7800
◪ As an "after-shopping or before-the-movies spot", this Chinese in Downtown's popular Horton Plaza mall is noted for its "generous portions" of "choice" items like honey walnut shrimp ("yes!"); wallet-watchers pronounce it "too pricey", but the majority points to the "pretty setting" and "extremely friendly staff."

Papachino's 🅂🅜   16 | 13 | 16 | $15
La Jolla Colony Shopping Ctr., 7748 Regents Rd. (north of Arriba St.), 619-546-7666
Flower Hill Mall, 2650 Via de la Valle (east of I-5), Del Mar, 619-481-7171
Parkway Plaza Mall, 627 Parkway Plaza (Johnson Ave.), El Cajon, 619-593-8500
13425 Poway Rd. (Community Rd.), Poway, 619-748-7100
◪ These suburban Italian "pizza joints" offer "good value" to a "young crowd" and even if the food is "just fair", it's convenient "before a movie" and "locals keep coming back" for the "basic", "affordable" fare.

Paper Moon Cafe ◑🅂🅜   ▽ 20 | 17 | 18 | $22
734 Fifth Ave. (bet. F & G Sts.), 619-544-6456
◼ Signaling a "change of pace in the Gaslamp Quarter", this "small bistro" with its "eclectic" Californian menu is a "yummy, more casual option"; if the room seems "a little crowded", the "romantic patio" affords a chance to enjoy the fresh air and eye the passersby.

Parioli Italian Bistro S M
▽ 23 | 18 | 21 | $27

647 S. Hwy. 101 (bet. Lomas Santa Fe Dr. & Via de la Valle), Solana Beach, 619-755-2525

■ "Real Italian" fare with "Euro flair" distinguishes this Solana Beach entry, a "great addition" to the area and a "pleasant surprise" with an "interesting menu", "friendly service" and a quiet, comfortable environment; local foodies cite this relative newcomer for its "tremendous potential."

Parkhouse Eatery S M
22 | 21 | 19 | $20

4574 Park Blvd. (bet. Madison & Monroe Aves.), 619-295-7275

■ A "quaint" "gem" in University Heights, this converted Victorian house boasts an Eclectic menu that can be "great fun", thanks to "zesty", "creative" cooking that reinterprets International favorites; throw in reasonable prices for "ample portions" and the trendy, Uptown clientele declares this "a good find."

Parrot Grill ◐
▽ 19 | 18 | 20 | $23

802 Sixth Ave. (F St.), 619-231-9981

◪ "Many dishes are unusual" at this Gaslamp Quarter American with a Caribbean accent; as the restaurant adjacent to the Tsunami Beach Club, it draws a party-loving crowd – "new and fun" is all that set needs to know.

Pasta Pronto S M
20 | 13 | 19 | $12

Albertson's Mall, 2673 Via de la Valle (east of I-15), Del Mar, 619-481-6017

■ The "cheap" prices at this Italian in Del Mar make it popular for "delicious and quick" pasta standards; though sparsely decorated, it offers "takeout supreme" and regulars will not leave without a slice of the "great mango tart."

Peking Palace S M
19 | 17 | 18 | $15

1400 Camino de la Reina (Mission Ctr. Rd.), 619-298-2181
University Towne Ctr., 4305 La Jolla Village Dr. (Genesee Ave.), 619-452-7500

◪ Noted for "consistent Chinese", this mall-based duo is praised for "good food and service" (though a minority protests the "ordinary" chow); they're a "favorite" among shoppers who value "quick lunches" and "fair prices" over culinary fireworks.

Peohe's Restaurant S M
19 | 25 | 20 | $30

Ferry Landing Mktpl., 1201 First St. (B Ave.), Coronado, 619-437-4474

◪ Supporters claim it's "worth the trip" for the "breathtaking" skyline view from this Coronado Pacific Rim powerhouse, which also earns applause for "enjoyable" food and its "one-of-a-kind" "Hawaiian theme" (think rain forests); however, vocal detractors insist it's "cheesy" and "touristy" and lament that the "novelty" is gone.

Peter & Harry's Restaurant Cafe S M
– | – | – | M

1201 Camino del Mar (Del Mar Heights Rd.), Del Mar, 619-509-8979

Sit on the comfortable, sheltered terrace at this Del Mar International newcomer with a heavy German accent and dig into chef Peter Windhovel's menu of hearty sandwiches, pastas and goulash, or sample such daily specials as German-style roast beef and pork.

P.F. CHANG'S CHINA BISTRO S M
21 | 21 | 18 | $22

4540 La Jolla Village Dr. (Executive Way), 619-458-9007

◪ "If you can get in", this "noisy", "fast-paced neo-Chinese" offers a "glitzy ambiance" and an "interesting menu" that's "a step above" the norm ("lettuce wraps are great"); it's popular with the dressy "to-be-seen crowd" that gravitates to this corner of the Golden Triangle, but authenticity nuts scoff at the "Americanized" approach.

Phil's Barbecue S M
– | – | – | I

4030 Goldfinch St. (Washington St.), 619-688-0559

Some of the "best barbecue in the region" makes this joint an "excellent addition to Mission Hills"; "very smoky", "awesome" classics like "ribs to die for" and "great chicken" draw fans, yet it's "more a take-out place than a restaurant", as it has only a few seats and even less decor; still, at these prices, nobody's complaining.

Pho Pasteur S M
▽ 20 | 11 | 15 | $12

7612 Linda Vista Rd. (Mesa College Dr.), 619-569-7515

■ This Linda Vista Vietnamese prides itself on "authentic" dishes ("don't miss the spring rolls") and a vast soup selection; given the "enjoyable food" and "reasonable prices", devotees focus on the "extensive" menu and forgive the limited decor.

Phuong Trang S M
23 | 9 | 14 | $14

4170 Convoy St. (Balboa Ave.), 619-565-6750

◪ The "fantastically large menu" ("take a dictionary") of "terrific Vietnamese" fare at this Convoy Street entry is so "cheap and good" that a "noisy, crowded atmosphere" is all but guaranteed; the kitchen works overtime to offset the "tacky setting" and the service that some describe as "not too friendly."

PIATTI S M
23 | 23 | 22 | $27

2182 Avenida de la Playa (2 blocks west of La Jolla Shores Dr.), La Jolla, 619-454-1589

■ Most tout this La Jolla Shores Italian as "a delight" for its "excellent, reliable menu" of pastas and other crowd-pleasers; the interior is an eyeful ("wonderful murals") and an earful ("loud"), but the "lovely patio" is an option "if you want to talk"; warm service "like a family friend" is a welcome touch, considering the meals are "not cheap."

Pick Up Stix 🆂Ⓜ
_| _| _| 1

10755 Scripps Poway Pkwy. (east of I-15), 619-547-0024
1040 University Ave. (10th Ave.), 619-295-7849
2508 El Camino Real (opp. Carlsbad Mall), Carlsbad, 760-720-6252
2710 Via de la Valle (opp. Flower Hill Mall), Del Mar, 619-259-7849
127 N. El Camino Real (Encinitas Blvd.), Encinitas, 760-632-8130
8707 Via La Jolla Dr. (Nobel Dr.), La Jolla, 619-552-1566
8025 Fletcher Pkwy. (Baltimore Dr.), La Mesa, 619-589-8191
1975 Garnet Ave. (Lamont St.), Pacific Beach, 619-483-9588
"Dependably" "fresh, fast Chinese food" at "cheap" tabs
is the winning formula of this chain; the, ahem, decor and
service could stand significant improvement, but legions
swear by these eateries for solid takeout.

Picoso 🆂
▽ 21 | 21 | 18 | $17

828 Prospect St. (Fay Ave.), La Jolla, 619-551-3232
■ "Casual" cantina that earns respect for its "tasty, fresh"
and "intensely flavorful" Mexican cooking and "charming"
decor; in sum, a "good addition to the La Jolla scene."

Pine Hills Lodge & Dinner Theatre 🆂Ⓜ
▽ 14 | 17 | 17 | $22

_Pine Hills Lodge, 2960 La Posada Way (Blue Jay Dr.),
Julian, 760-765-1100_
☑ "Go for the fun plays" and the "funky country setting"
because the "food is not the attraction" at this BBQ
outpost in Julian; it may be "rustic" and "something
different", but the ribs and chicken are hardly smokin'.

Pine Valley House 🆂Ⓜ
▽ 15 | 16 | 19 | $18

28841 Old Hwy. 80 (I-8), Pine Valley, 619-473-8708
☑ For "family dining" in a "rural setting" in the East County
backcountry, nostalgists turn to this vintage (opened 1927)
specialist in American home cooking; though it's "a step up"
from a coffee shop, the fare is "very average" and some
worry it may be "going downhill."

Pinnacle Peak Steakhouse 🆂Ⓜ
19 | 17 | 17 | $18

_7927 Mission Gorge Rd. (Rancho Fanita Dr.), Santee,
619-448-8882_
☑ The "cowboy atmosphere" at this veteran Santee
steakhouse strikes some as "totally silly", but the "original
ranch food" showcases enormous steaks at a right fair
price; the jeaned-and-booted gang appreciates the "down-
home" atmosphere and square "deal."

Pisces 🆂Ⓜ
_| _| _| E

_La Costa Resort & Spa, 2100 Costa Del Mar Rd. (El Camino Real),
Carlsbad, 760-438-9111_
After a day of cosseting at the La Costa spa in Carlsbad,
guests can continue to be pampered at this posh room on
the lower level; the "great menu" of "fine seafood" is "hard
to beat" and the old-world servers are true professionals,
but a few manage to sniff "overrated" nonetheless.

Pizza Bella [S][M] ▽ 22 | 15 | 19 | $10

2707 Congress St. (San Diego Ave.), 619-692-4333

■ Regulars give this low-key Old Towner its due for "great pizza", the standout on a menu that also features freshly made pasta; the "personable service" and budget prices hit the spot too.

Pizza Nova [S][M] 19 | 16 | 18 | $15

Village Hillcrest, 3955 Fifth Ave. (bet. University & Washington Aves.), 619-296-6682
5120 N. Harbor Dr. (Rosecrans St.), 619-226-0268
Grossmont Shopping Ctr., 5500 Grossmont Ctr. Dr., La Mesa, 619-589-7222
Lomas Santa Fe Plaza, 945 Lomas Santa Fe Dr. (I-5), Solana Beach, 619-259-0666

◪ Quartet of pizza-and-pasta houses that's a "favorite casual dining" experience, thanks to the wood-fired, "Nouvelle-style" "designer" pies – a "fun concept" featuring toppings like shrimp pesto; a few carp about "average", "chain-style" fare, but most are happy to sample "interesting" combos at a "moderate" cost.

Pizzeria Uno [S][M] 18 | 16 | 16 | $14

Fashion Valley Mall, 356 Fashion Valley (Friars Rd.), 619-298-1866
4465 Mission Blvd. (Hornblend St.), Pacific Beach, 619-483-4143 🌙

◪ Adherents of these chain pizzerias in Pacific Beach and the red-hot Fashion Valley Mall declare the Chicago-style "deep-dish delight" is "my kinda pizza" and revel in the "casual atmosphere", though foes rate the food "standard" and find the service a bit too informal; surf enthusiasts say "you can't beat the beach" location.

Planet Hollywood 🌙[S][M] 12 | 20 | 14 | $17

Horton Plaza, 197 Horton Plaza (bet. Broadway & 4th Ave.), 619-702-7827

◪ It may be "fun once" for the "neat", "glitzy" Tinseltown memorabilia, but this "commercialized" chain enterprise in Downtown's Horton Plaza gets an overall thumbs down for its "pitiful" American-Californian menu and "so-so" service; if "kids love" the "cute theme", their elders warn "bring the earplugs and shin guards."

Point Loma Seafoods [S][M]⇏ 24 | 12 | 16 | $12

2805 Emerson St. (Scott St.), 619-223-1109

■ "Sit outside" on the patio and enjoy the "wonderful eating" at this Point Loma seafood market/take-out joint (but beware the "cavorting seagulls" who are out to share your crab sandwich); it's "nothing fancy", but fans keep it "crowded" and the "employees are always hustling" to serve affordable, "good and fresh" fare ("squid sandwich rocks", "best seafood cocktails") to the lemming-like hordes who make this an "only in San Diego place."

Poseidon, The 🅂🅼 | 16 | 18 | 16 | $21 |
1670 Coast Blvd. (bet. 15th & 18th Sts.), Del Mar, 619-755-9345
☑ "Can't beat the location" say champions of this Del Mar beachsider, but most agree that the "good old high-calorie American fare" is no match for the "great view"; though the menu is just "adequate", the open-air deck is a fine "setting for a casual meal" and offers a "relaxing" spot to entertain "out-of-towners."

Postcards American Bistro 🅂🅼 ▽ | 14 | 14 | 15 | $17 |
Handlery Hotel, 950 Hotel Circle N. (I-8), 619-543-0607
■ The New American menu may be nothing to write home about, but it "will get you by" at this quiet, attractively decorated room in Mission Valley's Handlery Hotel; sizing up the clientele, dissenting locals offer faint praise: "good for package-tour food."

Prego 🅂🅼 | 22 | 21 | 20 | $25 |
Hazard Ctr., 1370 Frazee Rd. (Friars Rd.), 619-294-4700
■ "Especially for a chain", this "elegant" Tuscan villa–styled Mission Valley Italian has its "act together" when it comes to the "rich flavors" of its "well-prepared" cuisine; the "friendly staff" and "busy", "upscale" atmosphere give this "classy trattoria" its "solid" reputation – it's "just plain good for a business lunch."

Primavera Ristorante 🅂🅼 | 22 | 20 | 23 | $32 |
932 Orange Ave. (bet. 9th & 10th Sts.), Coronado, 619-435-0454
■ "Dark and elegant", this "cozy" Italian is known for serving "great food" that ranks among the "best" of its kind in Coronado; it's a "favorite local place for lunch" (albeit "expensive") and the dressy evening clientele eats up the "excellent" service.

Prince of Wales Grill 🅂🅼 | 22 | 24 | 23 | $39 |
Hotel del Coronado, 1500 Orange Ave. (R.H. Dana Pl.), Coronado, 619-522-8490
☑ A recent renovation has given this "sophisticated" room in the historic Hotel del Coronado a "beautiful new look", but surveyors can't concur whether the "expensive" New American cuisine is "pretty good" or "has gone downhill"; still, acolytes assert that this "special treat" is a "romantic" spot with "gracious" service.

Princess Pub & Grille 🅂🅼 | 19 | 22 | 21 | $27 |
1665 India St. (Date St.), 619-702-3021
■ "Bangers, mash and nostalgia" pack in throngs of expatriate Brits and other Commonwealth boosters at this "real English pub" in Little Italy; a "great bar" with a "limited menu" of "good pub grub" (specializing in fish 'n' chips), it's a "cozy room" with "character" and the "friendly" ambiance makes it a place "to take guests."

Putnam's Restaurant & Bar 🔲🔲 | 18 | 18 | 17 | $24
Colonial Inn, 910 Prospect St. (Girard Ave.), La Jolla,
619-454-2181
🔲 The "middle-of-the-road" American menu offered in the
handsomely decorated dining room at La Jolla's charming
Colonial Inn features "well-done entrees" and the "cozy",
"intimate" setting is a plus; however, a number of critics
deem it "basically ok" but "not memorable."

Quails Inn Dinner House 🔲🔲 | 17 | 19 | 18 | $19
1035 La Bonita Dr. (Rancho Sante Fe Rd.), San Marcos,
760-744-2445
🔲 Early-bird specials, buffets and a popular Sunday
brunch make this long-running American with a pleasantly
"unusual" lakeside setting in San Marcos a "seniors'
haven"; a moderately priced destination for "good food
and lots of it", it maintains a quiet atmosphere amid
"throwback-to-the-'70s" decor.

Qwiigs Bar & Grill 🔲🔲 | 20 | 20 | 18 | $23
5083 Santa Monica Ave. (Abbot St.), Ocean Beach,
619-222-1101
🔲 Named for the acronym invented by a '40s high school
fraternity ('Queeters who indulge in great sports'), this
"busy" second-story Ocean Beach seafood house boasts a
"gorgeous ocean view" and offers "fine" food and a
"great atmosphere" animated by a clientele of casually
clad "beach people"; doubters, though, find the service
"indifferent" and dub it a "hangout trying to be a restaurant."

RAINWATER'S ◐🔲🔲 | 25 | 22 | 24 | $38
1202 Kettner Blvd. (B St.), 619-233-5757
🔲 "Our version of Morton's of Chicago, but better" say
some San Diegans of this homegrown steakhouse, a
spacious, clubby "power location" "for a business lunch"
on the second floor of a restored building near the
Downtown waterfront; it pleases expense-account "big
shots" with "delicious beef" and a "wine room for
parties", but foes find it "stuffy" and "overrated."

Rancho El Nopal 🔲🔲 | 17 | 18 | 17 | $14
4016 Wallace St. (Calhoun St.), 619-295-0584
🔲 "Colorful" Mexican cafe offering "generous portions
of ordinary fare" and "pleasurable" "outdoor entertainment"
to a crowd that includes plenty of tourists; "we like the
authenticity" and "good margaritas" say supporters, but
despite the fair prices, detractors scoff at "unexceptional"
cuisine from "another unimaginative Old Town oldie."

RANCHO VALENCIA 🄢🄼

26 | 29 | 25 | $44

Rancho Valencia Resort, 5921 Valencia Circle (Rancho Diegueno Rd.), Rancho Sante Fe, 619-759-6216

■ Surveyors say "you can't beat the ambiance" at this smashingly "beautiful" room, part of the "exclusive" Rancho Valencia Resort near Rancho Santa Fe; besides "superb" Cal-Continental fare with Pacific Rim accents, it boasts a "great view", "leisurely service" and the "prettiest patio" on which to "lose the day"; in sum, well "worth the drive."

Red Sea 🄢🄼

▽ 20 | 10 | 20 | $18

4717 University Ave. (Euclid Ave.), 619-285-9722

■ A student favorite, this "authentic Ethiopian" in East San Diego features food that's "good in taste and value" and service that "strives to please"; it's not much to look at, but enthusiasts "enjoy it" for something "different."

Red Tracton's 🄢🄼

23 | 17 | 21 | $40

550 Via de la Valle (bet. Jimmy Durante Blvd. & Old Hwy. 101), Solana Beach, 619-755-6600

■ "Big steaks" at "big prices" rule at this "throwback-to-the-'50s" emporium noted for serving "voluminous amounts of food"; located across from the Del Mar racetrack, it attracts high rollers who relish the "great service", fine wine list and the atmospheric "dark" bar.

Restaurant Europa 🄢🄼

▽ 18 | 15 | 17 | $21

Oaktree Plaza, 9379 Mira Mesa Blvd. (bet. Black Mtn. Rd. & I-15), 619-693-3252

■ "For something different", this Mira Mesa German features a "festive atmosphere" and a "good European menu"; it's a hit with a mature crowd that likes their pork hock and beer served amid "dowdy", old-world decor while live piano music emanates from the bar.

Rhinoceros Cafe & Grill 🄢🄼

19 | 16 | 19 | $23

1166 Orange Ave. (Loma Ave.), Coronado, 619-435-2121

■ Convenient to the Lamb's Players Theatre, this "simple but stylish bistro" in Coronado tries to offer "something for everyone" on its Californian menu; it's a "solid" spot where the "lively atmosphere" and "pleasant" service may be bigger draws than the "basic" cooking.

Rimel's Rotisserie 🄢🄼

23 | 13 | 16 | $15

1030 Torrey Pines Rd. (Herschel Ave.), La Jolla, 619-454-6045

■ While the "chicken's great", the "fish is even better" at this "storefront" "local hangout" in La Jolla, where the faithful head for "outstanding, healthy", mesquite-smoked fare, including seafood that's "fresh-caught" by the owner; patrons can opt for "alfresco dining" or "perfect takeout."

Ristorante Michelangelo [S][M] ▽ 20 | 15 | 18 | $22
2806 Shelter Island Dr. (Shafter St.), 619-224-9478
■ The "ambitious menu" at this "regional Italian" near Shelter Island "hits the spot" according to acolytes who enthuse there's "so much to choose from, we love it" as much as its down-to-earth, "neighborhood" approach.

Roma Beach Caffe [S][M] 18 | 11 | 18 | $21
5737 La Jolla Blvd. (Bird Rock Ave.), La Jolla, 619-456-7477
◪ It's "like eating with family" at this "plucky" addition to La Jolla's Bird Rock restaurant row, a "quaint" "dive" that delivers "authentic Italian food"; the overall performance may be a little "uneven", but the "staff makes a valiant effort" and loyalists see "potential" in this "homey" spot.

Roppongi [S][M] – | – | – | M
875 Prospect St. (Fay Ave.), La Jolla, 619-551-5252
Sure, the menu at this clever Asian fusion in La Jolla lists entrees, but many opt for surprisingly affordable meals made from the tantalizing array of tapas, such as Mongolian duck quesadillas, the Dungeness crab stack and Korean-inspired barbecued ribs; done in rare woods and stone, the room is handsome, but be warned of the noise level.

Royal Thai Cuisine [S][M] 20 | 19 | 18 | $19
467 Fifth Ave. (Island Ave.), 619-230-8424
737 Pearl St. (Eads St.), La Jolla, 619-551-8424
■ "Reliable Thai" is the trademark of these La Jolla and Gaslamp sibs that offer a "large menu" of "consistently good", "spicy" favorites; "attentive service" and "attractive decor" complement the output from the kitchen, and the chefs will gladly make it "hot if you like."

Rubio's Baja Grill [S][M] 19 | 13 | 16 | $9
Hall of Justice, 330 W. Broadway, 1st fl. W. Wing Food Ct. (bet. State & Union Sts.), 619-338-8081
10460 Friars Rd. (Mission Gorge Rd.), 619-285-9985
Fashion Valley Mall, 7007 Friars Rd. (Camino de las Tiendas), 619-718-9976
3900 Fifth Ave. (University Ave.), 619-299-8873
901 Fourth Ave. (E St.), 619-231-7731
3555 Rosecrans St. (Midway Dr.), 619-223-2631
4504 E. Mission Bay Dr. (Garnet Ave.), 619-272-2801
Crossroads Shopping Ctr., 7420 Clairemont Mesa Blvd. (Ruffin Rd.), 619-268-5770
8935 Towne Ctr. Dr. (south of La Jolla Village Dr.), 619-453-1666
910 Grand Ave. (Cass St.), Pacific Beach, 619-270-4800
San Diego State University, 5157 College Ave. (Montezuma Rd.), 619-286-3844
■ "Good, healthy and quick" is all that true believers need to know about these ubiquitous Mexican fast-fooders that may be the "best casual concept in the U.S.A."; the "signature fish tacos" head a menu of "Baja specialties" that have "on-the-run" devotees declaring "gimme fins!"

Ruby's Diner [S][M] 17 | 18 | 17 | $12
Mission Valley Ctr., 1640 Camino del Rio N. (I-8), 619-294-7829
5630 Paseo del Norte (bet. Cannon Rd. & Car Country Dr.), Carlsbad, 760-931-7829
1 Pier View Way (Coast Hwy.), Oceanside, 760-433-7829
■ "Rock 'n' roll all day" at these "adorable diners" in Mission Valley, Carlsbad and Oceanside, the local outlets of a SoCal "hamburger-and-milk shake chain" with an all-American "fat food" outlook; they're "great for kids" and give elders an excuse to "relive childhood" in a "fun and nostalgic" "'50s setting."

Rusty Pelican [S][M] 18 | 18 | 18 | $22
4325 Ocean Blvd. (Grand Ave.), Pacific Beach, 619-274-3474
◪ The sunset dinners are "a good buy" at this seafood house on the boardwalk in Pacific Beach; but while fans feel that the food is "fresh and nicely prepared", cons contend that the "wholesome, ordinary" menu has a "very chainish" taste, adding that the "adequate fish choices" are "nothing special."

RUTH'S CHRIS STEAK HOUSE [S][M] 25 | 19 | 21 | $42
1355 N. Harbor Dr. (bet. Ash St. & Broadway), 619-233-1422
◪ "Maybe it's the butter" that the ultra-prime cuts are cooked in or maybe it's the kitchen's "great execution", but this cow palace near the Downtown waterfront "delivers" with "awesome sizzling steaks", so "elevating one's cholesterol was never such fun"; though detractors deem it "way expensive" and "overrated", it ranks high for serving "huge portions" of often "incredible" fare in a rowdy, "noisy" atmosphere.

Sadaf Restaurant [S][M] – | – | – | M
828 Fifth Ave. (bet. E & F Sts.), 619-338-0008
613 Pearl St. (Cuvier St.), La Jolla, 619-551-0643
"Aromatic, hearty Persian food" is the appeal of the "excellent" original branch in La Jolla and its "attractive" new offspring in Gaslamp; despite spotty service, diners are guaranteed a "full plate for their money."

Saffron Chicken [S][M] 23 | 9 | 16 | $11
3731-B India St. (Washington St.), 619-574-0177
Saffron Noodles & Saté [S]
3737 India St. (Washington St.), 619-574-7737
■ These Siamese twins are side-by-side establishments near Old Town – one specializes in "incredible" Thai roasted chicken and the other in "yummy" Thai noodles and "salad rolls to die for"; fans tout the "healthy" cooking and say they offer some of "the best takeout for the dollar", rendering the "no-decor" criticism moot.

Sally's 🅢🅜   22 | 23 | 20 | $32
Hyatt Regency Hotel, 1 Market Pl. (Harbor Dr.), 619-687-6080
■ This waterfront Downtowner "deserves recognition" for its striking "modern decor" and "lovely", seafood-heavy Mediterranean menu ("great crab cakes", the "best bouillabaisse") enhanced by "beautiful presentations and service"; a "special dinner" at the chef's table in the kitchen is a foodie's dream of a "great time", though "on a warm summer night", the patio is "the only way to go."

SALVATORE'S 🅢🅜   25 | 23 | 23 | $34
750 Front St. (G St.), 619-544-1865
■ This long-running, "classy" favorite in Downtown's most exclusive condominium tower produces "good, old-fashioned Northern Italian" fare in a "sophisticated", handsomely "rococo" setting; the "high-quality" kitchen is overseen by Raffaella Gangale while "charming" husband Salvatore plays host – so successfully that some think he "makes the experience."

Sammy's California Woodfired Pizza 🅢🅜   22 | 18 | 18 | $17
Horton Plaza, 720 Fourth Ave. (F St.), 619-230-8888
Park in the Valley, 1620 Camino de La Reina (Mission Ctr. Rd.), 619-298-8222
5970 Avenida Encinas (I-5 & Palomar Airport Rd.), Carlsbad, 760-438-1212
12925 El Camino Real (Del Mar Heights Rd.), Del Mar, 619-259-6600
702 Pearl St. (Draper Ave.), La Jolla, 619-456-5222
☑ "There's no pizza like Sammy's" say partisans of the "creative", Cal-style pies at this homegrown, "something-for-everybody" chain, which offers a "varied menu" and "a lot of food for the money"; the environment is "enjoyable" (even if "crowded" and "noisy"), but critics find fault with the "hit-or-miss" service.

Samson's 🅢🅜   15 | 13 | 15 | $14
La Jolla Village Ctr., 8861 Villa La Jolla Dr. (bet. La Jolla Village & Nobel Drs.), La Jolla, 619-455-1461
☑ Located in a La Jolla mall with seemingly "no competition for 10 miles", this newly renovated Jewish deli is "not of NY quality, but it's as close as you'll get here" say many mavens; in an "old-time atmosphere", a "slow" staff slings a "big variety" of "big sandwiches", breakfast standards and the like; the "food is average", but locals hope that the introduction of a new menu will be an improvement.

Samurai of Japan 🅢🅜   – | – | – | M
979 Lomas Santa Fe Dr. (east of I-5), Solana Beach, 619-481-0032
"Pleasant" and "a real find", this Solana Beach Japanese features "delicious" fare, notably at the "friendly bar" where the "excellent sushi" is "so fresh it wiggles"; in the dining room, expect speedy, if impersonal, service.

Sand Crab Cafe S M　　　▽ 17 | 13 | 13 | $18
*2229 Micro Pl. (bet. Barham Dr. & Opper St.), Escondido,
760-480-2722*
☑ "Whack 'em, crack 'em" at this "finger-licking mecca for
crabs" in Escondido, a "fun, sloppy", "funky stop" where
the servers "dump the shellfish directly on your table";
dainty detractors, however, "don't like the mess" and find
the fare too "spicy."

San Diego Brewing Co. S M　　17 | 16 | 19 | $16
10450 Friars Rd. (Mission Gorge Rd.), 619-284-2739
☑ "Nice but noisy", this modestly decorated brewpub
attracts a crowd who gathers mostly "for the beer, not the
food"; while the active bar offers one of the "best selections
of drafts in SD", the pub grub is merely "ok for a quick" meal.

San Diego Chicken Pie Shop S M ⊅　18 | 10 | 19 | $9
2633 El Cajon Blvd. (Oregon St.), 619-295-0156
■ A "local institution" and "perennial favorite", this "San
Diego tradition" that now calls North Park home dishes up
"cheap, good, fast" American "comfort food", namely the
"best chicken pies", "just like mom used to make" – "down-
home", "wholesome, filling" ("don't pay attention to the
calories"); "stick with" the house specialty, though, as the
"rest of the menu" leaves much to be desired.

San Diego Pier Cafe S M　　▽ 16 | 23 | 15 | $19
Seaport Village, 885 W. Harbor Dr. (Pacific Hwy.), 619-239-3968
☑ Set "on the water" at Downtown's tourist-packed Seaport
Village, this "quiet", attractive Californian has "location,
location, location" and a "great view" going for it; while
loyalists "love the spinach and Swiss cheese omelet" and
macadamia pancakes for breakfast and the fish 'n' chips
for lunch or dinner, the other items are just "fair" and for a
seafooder, most of the marine options are quite "average."

Sante ◑ S M　　　　　22 | 21 | 23 | $36
*7811 Herschel Ave. (bet. Silverado & Wall Sts.), La Jolla,
619-454-1315*
■ "Romantic and intimate", this "consistently excellent"
Italian on a quiet La Jolla side street is a "hidden gem", a
"great place with cozy hideaways" and a "fabulous" chef-
owner, Tony Buonsante, a "born host" who supervises a
"wonderful staff"; "the bar [with live piano music] and
patio [especially "delightful" at lunch] are most popular"
with regulars who appreciate the "traditional", if "pricey",
dishes that are "solidly executed."

Sardina's Italian S M　　　▽ 16 | 14 | 18 | $14
1129 Morena Blvd. (Buenos Ave.), 619-276-8393
■ "Excellent shrimp pasta" and "garlic cheese bread to
die for" headline the roster at this "inexpensive" Southern
Italian that's, let's say, erratically decorated, but serves
"good family meals" and bargain "two-for-one" dinner deals.

Saska's ◐ⓈⓂ
20 | 15 | 19 | $21

3768 Mission Blvd. (Redondo Ct.), Mission Beach, 619-488-7311

■ A "San Diego institution" that dates back to 1951, this "great dive" in Mission Beach has long specialized in "excellent steaks", seafood and "nothing fancy" yet "always good late-night fare" (the kitchen is open until 2 AM daily) and now, its new sushi bar is getting early praise ("so fresh"); P.S. beware the notorious "parking problems."

Sbicca ⓈⓂ
- | - | - | E

215 15th St. (Camino del Mar), Del Mar, 619-481-1001
Named for chef Susan Sbicca and her husband (and host) Dan, this unusual New American bistro in Del Mar rambles through assorted spaces until it reaches a rooftop terrace that affords a pleasant view; from the creative kitchen comes concoctions like grilled swordfish paired with a spicy wasabi-mustard sauce, black bean hummus and a terrine of polenta layered with wild mushrooms and sun-dried tomatoes.

Scalini ⓈⓂ
20 | 21 | 21 | $36

3790 Via de la Valle (El Camino Real), Del Mar, 619-259-9944
☑ "Upstairs, upscale, upper-brow" Northern Italian that's the "best place to see" "the who's who of San Diego", including the "beautiful people during Del Mar's racing season"; but many non-luminaries find the "overrated" "food too heavy" and "expensive" and object to the "pretentious" ambiance and "oppressive service."

Screens Bistro ⓈⓂ
▽ 15 | 19 | 17 | $17

Fashion Valley Mall, 7007 Friars Rd. (Hwy. 163), 619-697-1500
■ In hot, hot, hot Fashion Valley, this American yearling sports a unique decor that spotlights a panoply of video screens simultaneously broadcasting a wild assortment of TV programs, classic films, cartoons and more – a "great concept" say some, but others gripe that it "can be distracting while eating the mediocre food"; in any case, it's convenient to the 18-screen theater nearby.

Seau's ⓈⓂ
13 | 18 | 15 | $17

Mission Valley Ctr., 1640 Camino del Rio N. (Mission Ctr. Rd.), 619-291-7328
☑ Owned by San Diego Chargers linebacker Junior Seau, this "lively", "big barn of a sports bar in the Mission Valley Center" may be "great for watching ball games" (there's dozens of blaring TV monitors) and tossing back "cold beers", but most say that aside from the "pretty good burgers", the "uninspired" New American "bar food" is served by a "slow" staff that's "not too friendly."

Sevilla ◐ [S] [M] — 18 | 19 | 16 | $22
555 Fourth Ave. (Market St.), 619-233-5979
■ "Dark but inviting" with a "great Euro feel", this "authentic" "Spanish favorite" in the Gaslamp Quarter specializes in "paella at its best", "the best tapas in town" ("order lots and share") and "must-have sangria"; dinner comes with a "fun flamenco show", and afterwards on Tuesday and Thursday nights, dancing fools can "take free salsa lessons."

Sherman's [S] — – | – | – | I
7353 El Cajon Blvd. (73rd St.), La Mesa, 619-698-8797
Celebrated for its extensive Cajun-Creole buffet, this welcoming restaurant in quiet La Mesa offers one of the "best in town"; even if the "decor isn't great, it's not an issue" because the "delicious food at good-value" prices more than compensates.

Shien of Osaka [M] — – | – | – | M
The Plaza, 16769 Bernardo Ctr. Dr. (east of I-15), 619-451-0074
The "great sushi bar" at this Rancho Bernardo Japanese slices and dices "excellent" raw fish, but be advised that the "best choices are not on the menu" (let the sushi master compose for you); the cooked items are "delicious" and "clean"-tasting, and delivered by a "well-organized", if somewhat "aloof", staff.

Shores, The [S] [M] — 18 | 23 | 19 | $26
Sea Lodge Hotel, 8110 Camino del Oro (Avenida de la Playa), La Jolla, 619-456-0600
■ "We like the ambiance" at this "hidden gem right on the beach", not to mention the "fabulous view of the sun setting over the Pacific" from La Jolla's Sea Lodge Hotel; while the New American "food doesn't match" the "wow" setting, it's certainly "improving" – "delicious crab cakes" and "great fish" – making this "hideout" a fine, slightly "lower-cost alternative" to the nearby Marine Room (under the same ownership).

Siam [S] [M] — – | – | – | I
3545 Midway Dr. (Kemper St.), 619-523-5203
4451 University Ave. (Highland Ave.), 619-528-0949
Find some of the "best Thai in town" at these cheap, "underrated gems" in City Heights and the Midway district, where the authentic fare is spicy and generous.

Sirino's — ▽ 24 | 16 | 20 | $27
113 W. Grand Ave. (Broadway), Escondido, 760-745-3835
■ "God knows Escondido needs" this Classic French jewel – perhaps "the best north of town" – that charms diners with its "small-town ambiance" and "personal" service; the "amazing chef", Vincent Grumel, masterminds "outrageously wonderful, unique food" that's "consistently good" and the "early-bird dinner is a bargain."

Soup Exchange [S][M] 17 | 13 | 14 | $11

7095 Clairemont Mesa Blvd. (Shawline St.), 619-576-0622
285 Bay Blvd. (bet. E & F Sts.), Chula Vista, 619-585-9866
1840 Garnet Ave. (Lamont St.), Pacific Beach, 619-272-7766

◪ "Tasty" and "healthy" "salads aplenty" make this trio of "cafeteria"-like buffets a "great place for a quick and fresh meal", though many find the namesake soups merely "decent", if not "watery"; still, as it's "all-you-can-eat", it's "always a bargain for the big eater."

Souplantation [S][M] 19 | 14 | 16 | $11

17210 Bernardo Ctr. Dr. (Rancho Bernardo Rd.), 619-675-3353
6171 Mission Gorge Rd. (Vandever Ave.), 619-280-7087
Mira Mesa Mall, 8105 Mira Mesa Blvd. (Reagan Rd.), 619-566-1172
Piazza Carmel Shopping Ctr., 3804 Valley Ctr. Dr. (Carmel Valley Rd.), 619-481-3225
3960 W. Point Loma Blvd. (Midway Dr.), 619-222-7404
Plaza Camino Real, 1860 Marron Rd. (El Camino Real), Carlsbad, 760-434-9100
9158 Fletcher Pkwy. (Dallas St.), La Mesa, 619-462-4232

■ "Consistently good in its category", with a "variety of tasty soups" and "the biggest salad bar that I've ever seen", this "very clean", "terrifically managed" buffet chain is "a safe place to eat", making it "ideal for families"; you "get your money's worth here", so prepare for "a mob scene."

Spice & Rice Thai Kitchen [S][M] 23 | 21 | 21 | $15

7734 Girard Ave. (bet. Kline & Silverado Sts.), La Jolla, 619-456-0466

■ Voted the top Thai in SD, this "quick and friendly" "nice addition to La Jolla" serves a "great variety" of "delightful", "yummy" fare, including "excellent vegetarian selections" (try the "spicy basil noodles") in a "tiny" but "lovely" room to a youngish, hip crowd; a few detractors find the food a bit "bland", but regulars "love it every time we go there."

Spices Thai Cafe [S][M] 23 | 18 | 19 | $18

Piazza Carmel Shopping Ctr., 3810 Valley Ctr. Dr. (Carmel Valley Rd.), 619-259-0889
16441 Bernardo Ctr. Dr. (east of I-15), Rancho Bernardo, 619-674-4665

■ "Everyone should experiment" with the "creative", "fabulous Thai food" offered on the "varied menu" at this "always crowded" duo in Del Mar and Rancho Bernardo, where the "meals are beautifully choreographed ballets" and the "decor is soothing to the soul."

Spoons Grill & Bar [S][M] ▽ 15 | 14 | 15 | $12

2725 Vista Way (Hwy. 78), Oceanside, 760-757-7070

◪ The burgers and fries at this wallet-friendly, family American in Oceanside are "good" (though they come in "plastic baskets"), but most surveyors say "skip the rest" of the menu to avoid "bland food."

Sportsmen's Seafoods S M

| - | - | - | L |

1617 Quivira Basin Rd. (W. Mission Bay Dr.), 619-224-3551
Some say the "sandwiches are good" at this cheap, self-service fish market-cum-seafooder on Quivira Basin, but most feel that the "food has gone downhill"; "still, it's nice to sit outside and watch the boats and seagulls."

Star of India S M

| 19 | 15 | 17 | $20 |

423 F St. (bet. 4th & 6th Aves.), 619-544-9891
Piazza Carmel Shopping Ctr., 3860 Valley Ctr. Dr. (El Camino Real), 619-792-1111
1000 Prospect St. (Girard Ave.), La Jolla, 619-459-3355
☑ You "can't beat the buffet lunch" at this trio of traditionally decorated Indians around town, which offers "great chicken korma" and curries, as well as "lots of options for vegetarians"; the staff "accommodates requests", but detractors find the "overpriced" food "too greasy."

St. Germain's Cafe S M

| 18 | 13 | 16 | $12 |

1010 Old Hwy. 101 (I St.), Encinitas, 760-753-5411
■ "Delightfully relaxing" despite "cramped seating" and "uneven service", this American in laid-back Encinitas is known for its "wonderful baking" and is one of "my favorite breakfast places" ("good omelets"); the outdoor "patio is great for lunches" ("interesting, tasty sandwiches" and soups), but it's not open for dinner.

St. James Bar & Restaurant M

| 20 | 22 | 21 | $31 |

4370 La Jolla Village Dr. (Executive Way), 619-453-6650
■ For "power-dining in La Jolla", many VIPs meet at this "sophisticated" Continental for a "fine" business lunch and order the "awesome mussel bisque" "every time" from an "excellent", "inventive" menu served by an "attentive staff" in a "lovely" room; some reviewers, however, "liked it better" when this site was known as Triangles, citing "superior" fare and a less "limited" selection.

Stuart Anderson's Black Angus S M

| 17 | 16 | 17 | $19 |

10750 Camino Ruiz (Mira Mesa Blvd.), 619-693-3453
10370 Friars Rd. (Mission Gorge Rd.), 619-563-5862
5247 Kearny Villa Rd. (Clairemont Mesa Blvd.), 619-279-3100
3340 Sports Arena Blvd. (Rosecrans St.), 619-223-5604
707 E St. (bet. I-5 & Broadway), Chula Vista, 619-426-9200
1000 Graves Ave. (Broadway), El Cajon, 619-440-5055
2471 Vista Way (El Camino Real), Oceanside, 760-433-7712
☑ "When you want a decent steak at a decent price", head to this chain of "loud and dark", "hunk-o-meat places" that also feature "surprisingly good" prime rib and "bargain specials"; even so, critics counter that this "moo city" serves "unmemorable" eats, adding that "management never has enough servers."

Su Casa [S][M] 16 | 16 | 16 | $16

6738 La Jolla Blvd. (Playa del Norte), La Jolla, 619-454-0369

◪ Though the "decor is tired" at this "cozy and busy" La Jolla Mexican, the "fun" atmosphere makes it a "hangout for families and surfers from Windansea Beach"; insiders insist that "the taco tray and guacamole made at the table are a must", but foes complain about "heavy", "inauthentic" dishes and "almost nonexistent service."

Sushi on the Rock [S][M] 24 | 15 | 18 | $21

7734 Girard Ave. (Silverado St.), La Jolla, 619-456-1138

■ "Even if you don't love sushi" – and that's the only type of fare served at this La Jolla Japanese – the "upbeat atmosphere" and recorded rock music that gives it its name make this a "fun sushi bar for young people"; of course, for foodies there's just the pure allure of "inventive" raw fish.

SUSHI OTA [S][M] 27 | 13 | 17 | $26

4529 Mission Bay Dr. (Balboa Ave.), 619-270-5670

■ Despite an "odd location" near the freeway at the backside of Pacific Beach, this Japanese shrine is "always crowded" because the chef is an "artist with a knife", turning out "creative" sushi that's "the best in San Diego"; the food is so good that "visitors from Tokyo specifically request" a visit here, and it more than makes up for "lunch-counter decor" and "inconsistent service."

Swadee Thai Restaurant [S][M] ▽ 22 | 18 | 21 | $18

1001 C Ave. (10th St.), Coronado, 619-435-8110

■ Coronado locals "love" this "darling" Thai newcomer that's staffed by "nice, nice, nice" servers who "care" and chefs who prepare "outstanding", "wonderful food."

Sze Chuan [S][M] ▽ 21 | 16 | 18 | $15

4577 Clairemont Dr. (Clairemont Mesa Blvd.), 619-270-0251

■ "Creative concoctions of Szechuan and Mandarin dishes", "spicy" and "excellently" executed, account for the popularity of this Clairemont Chinese; it's a bit of a "dive", but "great lunch combos" and "fair prices" make it a "favorite take-out" choice.

Taco Auctioneer [S][M] 17 | 14 | 18 | $14

1951 San Elijo Ave. (Birmingham Dr.), Cardiff-by-the-Sea, 760-942-8226

■ "Practical jokes abound" at this "funky" Mexican in Cardiff-by-the-Sea, where the waiters serve up "lots of fun", along with a "great taco plate" and "excellent *carnitas*"; that's enough for boosters who believe that this is the home of "the original happy meal", but others sigh "sometimes the food is inspired, but who knows when?"; still, it's one of the "best beer and sunset places around."

Tajima [S] – | – | – | I
4681 Convoy St. (Clairemont Mesa Blvd.), 619-576-7244
Enjoy "good", authentic fare served by a pleasant staff at this tiny but comfortable and inexpensive Japanese on the Convoy Street Asian restaurant row in Kearny Mesa.

TAKA [S][M] 26 | 19 | 21 | $29
555 Fifth Ave. (Market St.), 619-338-0555
■ The "trendy" young things who populate the Gaslamp Quarter agree that this is the "best" and "hippest" Downtown sushi bar, and its Asian fusion menu offers a "superb" alternative to the Italian fare that dominates the neighborhood; while the claim that "beautiful folks" get top treatment is open to debate, there's no denying the "long lines", so hunker down.

Tapenade [S] – | – | – | E
7612 Fay Ave. (bet. Kline & Pearl Sts.), La Jolla, 619-551-7500
Jean-Michel and Sylvie Diot left behind successful restaurants in NY for sunny SD, and their new venture, which opened in La Jolla in summer '98, has drawn early raves from fans who call it the "best new French" and predict it "will be big"; offering a seafood-heavy bistro menu in a breezy, South of France–like setting, it's fairly "pricey", but the well-heeled clientele doesn't seem to mind.

Taste of Thai [S][M] 21 | 17 | 19 | $17
527 University Ave. (bet. 5th & 6th Aves.), 619-291-7525
15770 San Andres Dr. (Via de la Valle), Del Mar, 619-793-9695
■ These "popular" Siamese twins in Hillcrest and Del Mar are "always crowded" because they offer "consistently good food at great prices", especially "big portions" of "yummy pad Thai" and "excellent vegetarian choices"; the "service is sometimes slow", but regulars promise that this "treat for the palate" is "worth the wait."

TD Hays [S][M] 19 | 18 | 18 | $20
4315 Ocean Blvd. (Grand Ave.), Pacific Beach, 619-270-8747
◪ Perched on the boardwalk in Pacific Beach, this casual, second-story steak-and-seafood house affords "awesome views" that make "trusty" dinners even more satisfying ("delicious prime rib" and "good fish"); critics, however, find the "basic menu nothing special" and say the "run-down" room "needs a face-lift."

Terra [S][M] – | – | – | E
1270 Cleveland Ave. (Vermont St.), 619-293-7088
A soothing interior serves as sharp contrast to Neil Stuart's wildly innovative cuisine that's based on unusual combinations and spicy undertones at this new Pan Asian–New American in Hillcrest; the chef takes plenty of risks, betting that his clientele will share his passion for experimentation; even if not all the concoctions work, the nifty wine list makes everything easier to swallow.

T.G.I. Friday's ◐ⓈⓂ `15` `16` `16` `$16`

403 Camino del Rio S. (Mission Ctr. Rd.), 619-297-8443
Carmel Mtn. Plaza Shopping Ctr., 11650 Carmel Mtn. Rd.
(Rancho Carmel Dr., 1 block east of I-15), Carmel Mtn. Ranch,
619-675-7047
8801 Villa La Jolla Dr. (Nobel Dr.), La Jolla, 619-455-0880
☑ "Noisy" Traditional American chain with an "active
atmosphere" whose happy hour draws a "fun crowd";
but while its "uncontrollably huge" lineup of dishes has
"something for everyone", detractors gripe that its
"programmed menu is a tired concept", as is its "dated
'70s circus decor."

Thaigo ⓈⓂ ▽ `18` `16` `19` `$12`

Carmel Mtn. Plaza Shopping Ctr., 11720 Carmel Mtn. Rd.
(Highland Ranch Rd.), Carmel Mtn. Ranch, 619-675-8188
☑ Tucked into a Carmel Mountain Ranch mall, this simple
Thai semi–fast-fooder has an "interesting", "good-deal"
menu, but surveyors say the fare is "uneven" (and can be
"very, very spicy") due to its "assembly-line" production.

Thai House Cuisine Ⓜ `22` `16` `22` `$15`

4225 Convoy St. (bet. Aero Dr. & Balboa Ave.), 619-278-1800
■ Not only is the cuisine "authentic" at this Convoy Street
Thai, but the food is so "delicious" ("spring rolls to die for"
and a wide array of vegetarian offerings) and "well-
presented" that some quibble about "small portions"; P.S.
the "fast" staff "treats you like family."

Thai Orchid Cuisine ⓈⓂ ▽ `15` `15` `17` `$14`

4310 Genesee Ave. (Mt. Etna Dr., 1 block north of Balboa Ave.),
Clairemont, 619-278-4949
■ The few who frequent this "hideaway" in Clairemont say
it provides a "peaceful background for consuming pad
Thai" and other "ok, not too spicy" fare at budget prices.

THEE BUNGALOW ⓈⓂ `25` `19` `23` `$34`

4996 W. Point Loma Blvd. (Bacon St.), 619-224-2884
☑ For more than a decade, chef Edmund Moore has
followed a successful recipe blending generous portions,
hearty French cuisine and reasonable prices at this
"excellent standby" in an "old Ocean Beach house"; the
older "regular crowd" sings the praises of the "best roast
duck", "bargain" early-bird menu and "fantastic" value
wine list, drowning out the few who think the food's too
"heavy" and the decor "needs updating."

Tin Ching ⓈⓂ `-` `-` `-` `I`

859 Hornblend St. (bet. Garnet & Grand Aves.), Pacific Beach,
619-272-0930
While some locals say the food at this "traditional,
neighborhood Chinese" in Pacific Beach can be "tasty"
("good fried rice and orange chicken"), critics counter
that it's "disappointing"; it will have to be your call here.

Tom Ham's Lighthouse 🗑️ Ⓜ️   13 | 18 | 16 | $21
2150 Harbor Island Dr. (Harbor Dr.), 619-291-9110
■ "Tourists get a marvelous view" of the city at this spacious American located at the tip of Harbor Island, but that "doesn't make up for" the "'70s red vinyl/red carpet" decor that's as "out of date as the food"; still, as it's such a "pretty spot", some come for the "decent" lunch buffet, a "better" choice than the "boring" à la carte dinner.

Tony Roma's 🗑️ Ⓜ️   17 | 14 | 17 | $18
Promenade Shopping Ctr., 4110 Mission Blvd. (Pacific Beach Dr.), Pacific Beach, 619-272-7427
1814 Marron Rd. (Jefferson St.), Carlsbad, 760-720-0700
Target Shopping Ctr., 8111 Mira Mesa Blvd. (Camino Ruiz), Mira Mesa, 619-695-6500
1020 W. San Marcos Blvd. (Via Vera Cruz), San Marcos, 760-736-4343
☑️ "Always noisy and crowded", this "family-oriented" barbecue chain cooks up "good ribs for the price" and "onion rings to die for"; while the menu offers a "nice variety" of basics, most say that the babybacks "are the best bet"; it's a "great deal for the money", but purists sniff "big portions, small taste" and complain too of "slow" service and "decor that needs updating."

Tony's Jacal 🗑️ Ⓜ️   20 | 15 | 19 | $16
621 Valley Ave. (Stevens Ave.), Solana Beach, 619-755-2274
■ "Viva Mexico" at this "favorite" old-timer in Solana Beach, one of the most "authentic" "north of the border" and still "popular" for "the best fish tacos in the country", "great *chile rellenos*", "unusual refried beans" and "good margaritas" delivered in "comfortable surroundings."

TOP OF THE MARKET 🗑️ Ⓜ️   25 | 24 | 23 | $33
750 N. Harbor Dr. (Broadway), 619-234-4867
■ "Ask for a corner window table" at this "upscale", "special-occasion" seafood palace with a "gorgeous view" of San Diego Bay; it's a "great setting" for "always top-notch" fish ("try the John Dory – wow" or the "wonderful ahi") that's served by an "informed" staff; it's "expensive", but the dining experience is "a treat" that's "well worth the price every time."

TOP O' THE COVE 🗑️ Ⓜ️   24 | 26 | 23 | $42
1216 Prospect St. (Ivanhoe Ave.), La Jolla, 619-454-7779
☑️ Expect to be "pampered in luxury" at this "sophisticated", "elegant Continental" "class act"; it may be "pricey", but its "lovely view" of La Jolla Cove is "romantic" and chef Guy Sockrider's "superb" cuisine is complemented by a "fine wine list"; despite attentive service, however, many object to the "snooty" staff and and "snobby atmosphere"

Torreyana Grille [S][M] 21 22 20 $31

Hilton La Jolla Torrey Pines, 10950 N. Torrey Pines Rd. (Science Park Dr.), La Jolla, 619-450-4571

◪ Near the close of '98, chef Deborah McDonald Schneider took over the range at this lovely New American–Californian in La Jolla, thus outdating the above food rating; while the venue serves as a "breakfast hangout for business" types, it's also a "good choice for Sunday brunch" and the same "wonderful staff" takes care of all the details.

Torrey Pines Cafe [S][M] 19 16 18 $23

2334 Carmel Valley Rd. (Via Donada), Del Mar, 619-259-5878

■ The younger sibling of the Bird Rock Cafe, this "casual", local "favorite" near Del Mar features a "refreshingly different" New American–International menu with "some dishes that will knock your socks off", like "pure, sweet mussels from the owner's farm" and "perfect pasta", along with such "well-prepared" "comfort foods" as "super meat loaf"; as a plus, most dishes come with a "plate-size option" of mini or maxi portions.

TRATTORIA ACQUA [S][M] 24 24 21 $30

Coast Walk, 1298 Prospect St. (Coast Blvd.), La Jolla, 619-454-0709

■ If you're lucky enough to get a "seat in the gazebo", you'll revel in "delightful outdoor dining overlooking La Jolla Cove" at this "ever-so-popular" "jewel", voted one of the top Italians in San Diego; indoors, the "setting is beautiful" too, with a "charming atmosphere" and an "accommodating staff" that serves an "ambitious", "innovative" menu of "sublime" creations from chef Joseph Savino and "an unbelievable array of wines" (more than 500 selections); in all, it's "romantic, delicious and well-priced – what else could you ask for?"

Trattoria Fantastica [S][M] 20 19 18 $21

1735 India St. (Date St.), 619-234-1735

■ An offspring of the popular Busalacchi's Ristorante, this "family-owned Italian" in Little Italy is a "charming" "neighborhood place" where the staff "tries hard" to please with "delicious", "reasonably priced" fare served in an "authentic trattoria setting" and out on the "nice patio."

Trattoria La Strada ☾[S][M] 20 21 20 $26

702 Fifth Ave. (G St.), 619-239-3400

◪ A "big, popular trattoria in Gaslamp", this Italian is "another good" entry among many competitors on Fifth Avenue; admirers find it "reliable" for "old-world" dishes, and the "streetside" patio makes it a "people-watching" favorite when the jammed interior gets too "noisy", but dissenters dismiss it as a "tourist place."

Trattoria Mannino 🖪🅼   20 | 17 | 18 | $23

5662 La Jolla Blvd. (Bird Rock Ave.), La Jolla, 619-551-8610

📩 "Small and reasonable", this "overlooked gem" with a "bistro atmosphere" in La Jolla's Bird Rock neighborhood serves the "best cannelloni in San Diego", along with other "consistently good" meals; despite visions of "mama in the kitchen" preparing dishes that are "better than my fantasies" of Italian cuisine, a few find the fare "heavy"; N.B. for music lovers, there's live jazz and blues.

Trattoria Portobello 🖪🅼   23 | 20 | 21 | $30

715 Fourth Ave. (bet. F & G Sts.), 619-232-4440

📩 "Fantastic" appetizers almost "keep me from ordering entrees" at this "excellent Italian" in the Gaslamp Quarter, "among the best" purveyors of Northern specialties in town – the namesake mushrooms are indeed "fabulous" and the "bocconcini are super"; an interesting martini bar, chic decor and a "quiet" ambiance make some think it's "perfect for a date", though skeptics say it's "undistinguished."

Trattoria Positano 🖪🅼   23 | 18 | 20 | $28

2171 San Elijo Ave. (Chesterfield), Cardiff-by-the-Sea, 760-632-0111

142-G University Ave. (3rd Ave.), 619-294-6995

◼ It's easy to see why early admirers dub this "wonderful, boisterous" Cardiff-by-the-Sea newcomer "a future star"; thanks to "impressive renditions of authentic" cuisine, "friendly" service, "beautiful decor", a "delightful mood" and an ocean view, it's already one of the best Italians in the county and many "hope it stays" around for a long time; N.B. a new branch has just opened in Hillcrest.

Trophy's 🖪🅼   17 | 18 | 18 | $17

Costa Verde Ctr., 4282 Esplanade Ct. (bet. Genesee Ave. & La Jolla Village Dr.), 619-450-1400

7510 Hazard Ctr. Dr. (Friars Rd. & Hwy. 163 at Frazee Rd.), 619-296-9600

Grossmont Shopping Ctr., 5500 Grossmont Ctr. Dr. (I-8 & Jackson Dr.), La Mesa, 619-698-2900

📩 The American fare – "great salads", "wonderful white bean chili", wood-fired pizzas, sandwiches and burgers – is "actually pretty good" at this trio of "loud", "fun sports bars" decorated with vast displays of "memorabilia" and "lots of TVs" for "watching the ball games"; nonfans, though, complain that the "boring" "food needs work."

Tupelo 🖪🅼   18 | 22 | 19 | $25

340 Fifth Ave. (bet. J & K Sts.), 619-231-3140

📩 Perhaps the "best martinis in town" can be sipped at this "pretty" Californian newcomer in Gaslamp, where the "bartender can make more than 100 different" versions (the chocolate one rates a "wow"); however, many feel that the bistro is "still in the growing stage", producing mostly "disappointing" fare, and the service "needs improvement."

TUTTO MARE 🗴🗴 23 | 22 | 21 | $29
4365 Executive Dr. (Genesee Ave.), 619-597-1188
☑ By day, this spacious, "high-tech Italian" seafooder in the Golden Triangle is a "reliable" "power-lunch hangout" populated by "suits" and "attentive" servers; at night, "be sure to wear black to fit in" with the "noisy," trendy "pretty people" who jam the tables to enjoy "imaginative" dishes ("don't miss the lobster-and-crab pasta") and "great live [jazz and classical] music."

Valentino's 🗴🗴 – | – | – | M
Mercado, 11828 Rancho Bernardo Rd. (Rancho Bernardo Ctr. Dr.), 619-451-3200
Named after the silent screen matinee idol, this Rancho Bernardo Northern Italian features a romantic atmosphere at night when a live trio performs most evenings; by day, it's a favored destination for business lunchers who enjoy "solid" renditions of fettuccine with shrimp and scallops or grilled ahi with rosemary, served by waiters who are efficient, if "pretentious."

Vegetarian Zone 🗴🗴 20 | 12 | 17 | $16
2949 Fifth Ave. (Quince St.), 619-298-7302
☑ "A vegan's dream", this "groovy" Hillcrest spot provides "lots of choices" of "wonderful", "flavorful" entrees that are "healthy, healthy, healthy" (though some regulars wish it would "put something new on the menu"); nonbelievers counter that "the small portions" are "hardly tasty" and the decor "too '60s."

Venetian Restaurant 🗴🗴 20 | 16 | 20 | $17
3663 Voltaire St. (Chatsworth Blvd.), Ocean Beach, 619-223-8197
■ For "blue-collar Italian at its best", head to this neighborhood standby in Ocean Beach, an "old-time favorite" that makes "awesome pizza" (the tomato-and-garlic version is "superb") and "basic but consistent stuff" like "great linguine with clams"; "eat on the back patio" to really soak up the lively beach atmosphere.

Vesuvio Gourmet 🗴🗴 ▽ 22 | 16 | 16 | $16
3025 El Cajon Blvd. (30th St.), 619-282-3636
■ "In a neighborhood that needs a quality Italian bargain", this "delightful, tucked-away find" in North Park fits the bill with "large portions of traditional" fare ("yummy veggie pizza") delivered in a casual, relaxing atmosphere.

Via Italia Trattoria 🗴🗴 – | – | – | M
Clairemont Town Sq. Shopping Ctr., 4705 Clairemont Dr. (Clairemont Mesa Blvd.), 619-274-9732
While not yet widely known, this Italian newcomer in Clairemont Town Square is already a "diamond", offering an experience that's "like being in Italy"; "superior food", comfortable surroundings and warm service make it "much more than a pizzeria."

Vicino Mare [S] [M] 20 | 17 | 20 | $27
1702 India St. (Date St.), 619-702-6180
■ "Attentive chef" Lydia Simonette takes an "interesting slant on Italian food" and prepares "simple" "seafood at its finest" at this "excellent new find" in Little Italy, courtesy of the busy Busalacchi family; expect a "small, cute room" with a soothing, sea-themed decor and "friendly" staff.

Vigilucci's Pizzeria Italiana [S] [M] 22 | 16 | 19 | $21
1933 San Elijo Ave. (Birmingham Dr.), Cardiff-by-the-Sea, 760-634-2335
■ Take in a "sunset on the porch" and a lovely "view of the Pacific" at this "beachy" Cardiff-by-the-Sea Italian while savoring "food that's always good" – "delicious pizza" that's among the best in SD and "truly outstanding daily fish specials", served by an "accommodating" and "pleasant" (if sometimes too "laid-back") staff.

Vigilucci's Trattoria Italiana [S] [M] 22 | 16 | 20 | $25
505 S. Coast Hwy. 101 (D St.), Encinitas, 760-942-7332
◪ "Wow! we stopped by on a whim and what a surprise" to find Italian food so "excellent" that it "would make the chefs in the film *Big Night* proud"; this "great local spot" in a "funky" Encinitas setting is the older, less casual sibling of the similarly named pizzeria and regulars warn "be prepared to wait for a table" at this "tiny place", though it's "worth it"; still, a minority are unimpressed with "mediocre" fare, "tight seating" and "not-too-elegant" decor.

Vignola [S] [M] ▽ 26 | 20 | 24 | $34
St. James Hotel, 828 Sixth Ave. (bet. E & F Sts.), 619-231-1111
■ Though too new to be widely known by surveyors, this simply but pleasantly decorated newcomer, which opened on the fringe of the sizzling Gaslamp Quarter in spring '98, is earning early praise for its "awesome foie gras" and "innovative French fare" from "hot" chef Fabrice Poigin, who is warmly remembered from previous stints around town; "reasonable prices" and a smoothly trained young staff are pluses.

Vivace [S] [M] 22 | 25 | 21 | $41
Four Seasons Resort Aviara, 7100 Four Seasons Point (bet. Aviara Pkwy. & Poinsettia Ln.), Carlsbad, 760-603-6999
◪ This "beautiful" Northern Italian in Carlsbad's new, striving-for-five-stars Four Seasons Resort Aviara earns a warm reception as a "welcome addition" to the North County scene; though the well-heeled suburbanites who flock to this "elegant" enclave express some reservations (at these prices, they "need to work harder on the food"), the more lenient note that it's "still new" and improving.

When in Rome 🇸Ⓜ
22 | 20 | 20 | $30

1108 S. Hwy. 101 (J St.), Encinitas, 760-944-1771

☑ The "pasta is supreme" – particularly the "wonderful ravioli" and "terrific three-pasta sampler" – at this "romantic" Italian in a "gorgeous" villa-like setting in Encinitas; "one of the top spots for a special evening", it showcases "rather formal Italian cooking" that's "solid", if "heavy"; cynics sniff it's "not as good as when we were in Rome."

WINESELLAR & BRASSERIE 🇸
27 | 20 | 25 | $42

*9550 Waples St. (bet. Mira Mesa Blvd. & Steadman St.),
619-450-9557*

■ Douglas Organ is too old now to be the *enfant terrible* of San Diego chefs, but his casually chic New French "hidden gem" in Sorrento Mesa remains a true "original" that's "worth a trip to the warehouse district", offering "the best marriage of food and wine", as well as "attentive service"; some find it "too expensive for the decor", but with 3,000 wines to choose from and a six-variety tasting every Saturday (lunch optional), it's "heaven" for oenophiles.

Wolfgang Puck Cafe 🇸Ⓜ
19 | 17 | 17 | $21

*Mission Valley Ctr., 1640 Camino del Rio N. (Mission Ctr. Rd.),
619-295-9653*

☑ Despite the direction of celebrity chef Wolfgang Puck, this "trendy" Californian newcomer in "an odd mall location" in Mission Valley has "chain" written all over it because of a "deafening noise level" that nearly overwhelms the "good but not great" fare – "interesting pizzas, pastas" and salads; while many say they "wouldn't go out of my way to eat here", shoppers find it "convenient" (though "overpriced") for "casual dining."

World Curry 🇸Ⓜ
‒ | ‒ | ‒ | I

*1433 Garnet Ave. (bet. Gresham & Haines Sts.),
619-270-4455*

A tasty world of Indian, Thai and Japanese curries highlights the "many unique menu choices" at this "casual", "best-kept secret in Pacific Beach"; in particular, the "chicken panang is to die for", but regulars urge "try them all."

World Famous 🇸Ⓜ
19 | 18 | 18 | $19

*Boardwalk, 711 Pacific Beach Dr. (Mission Blvd.),
619-272-3100*

☑ Long celebrated as a "great hangout" right on the boardwalk in Pacific Beach, this "classic" American seafood house features "incredible fish", the "best lobster tacos" and a popular happy hour that makes it a "good, local gathering place"; dissenters, however, gripe about food and service that are "constantly inconsistent."

Yakitori II 🇸🇲 | 22 | 17 | 19 | $18 |

Sports Arena Village Shopping Ctr., 3740 Sports Arena Blvd. (Midway Dr.), 619-223-2641

■ Though the "service and decor need work", this quiet Japanese in the Sports Arena district is praised by many locals for its "good variety" of "clean-tasting", "delicious" dishes like the "enjoyable" sushi, seared ahi and "great salad" (the "garlic dressing alone is worth the trip"), but some find the "small portions" "too gringo-ized."

Yen's Wok on Pearl 🇸🇲 | 20 | 14 | 21 | $19 |

915 Pearl St. (bet. Fay & Girard Aves.), La Jolla, 619-456-1414

■ With "sweet" owners who are "always there to greet your family" and an "excellent", wide-ranging Asian menu influenced by Chinese, Korean and Japanese cuisines ("great Peking duck", bulgogi, "fresh, if not very creative, sushi"), this "wonderful" La Jolla spot attracts a local crowd that doesn't mind the "bare-bones" decor; P.S. it's one of the "best take-out" options in the area.

Yoshino 🇸 ∇ | 15 | 13 | 17 | $13 |

1790 W. Washington St. (India St.), 619-295-2232

☑ This standby near Old Town offers perhaps the "best value in San Diego", serving "huge portions" of traditional Japanese fare, including a limited selection of sushi that can be "incredible" but is more often only "average."

Yummy Maki Yummy Box 🇸🇲 ∇ | 15 | 9 | 16 | $13 |

3211 Holiday Ct. (Villa La Jolla Dr.), La Jolla, 619-587-9848

■ "Different and good", this modest, family-owned La Jolla "treasure" is a "college hangout" popular for "filling" Japanese food like "great, cheap noodles and California rolls", despite "low-bid decor" and minimal atmosphere.

Zagarella 🇸🇲 | 21 | 12 | 20 | $16 |

1655 India St. (bet. Cedar & Date Sts.), 619-236-8764

■ Imbued with a "cozy, family feel", this "neighborhood Italian" in Little Italy ladles up "excellent minestrone" and "cooks to order" such "homestyle" dishes as "fresh, tasty pasta" and "good veal"; both office workers and locals value its quiet atmosphere and accommodating service.

Zeena's Mediterranean 🇸🇲 | – | – | – | I |

558 Fourth Ave. (Market St.), 619-238-5238

Don't miss the Middle Eastern beef *shawarma* sandwich at this attractive, brightly-lit Mediterranean newcomer in the Gaslamp Quarter that's influenced by many cultures; other specialties of the house include Moroccan *b'steeya*, calamari salad, braised lamb shank and wood-fired pizzas with a twist (try the one topped with duck confit).

Indexes to Restaurants

Special Features and Appeals

CUISINES

Afghan
Kabul West
Khyber Pass

American (New)
Adam's Ave. Grill
Baily Wine Country
Bird Rock Cafe
Brockton Villa
Cafe Champagne
Cafe on Park
Cafe 222
Chino
Cody's
Cottage
Crescent Shores
Dining Room
Dobson's
Fifth & Hawthorne
George's at the Cove
Humphrey's
Inn at the Park
Jake's
Kensington Grill
La Valencia
L'Escale
Market Cafe
Mission
150 Grand Café
Pacifica Del Mar
Pacific Coast Grill
Pamplemousse Grille
Parrot Grill
Planet Hollywood
Postcards
Prince of Wales
Putnam's
Sbicca
Seau's
Shores
Terra
Torreyana Grille
Torrey Pines Cafe

American (Traditional)
Adam's Steak & Eggs
Albie's Beef Inn
Beach House
Bennigan's
Big Kitchen
Buffalo Joe's
Bully's
Butcher Shop

Callahan's Pub
Cass Street B&G
Cecil's Cafe
Claim Jumper
Corvette Diner
Crest Cafe
Dick's Last Resort
Dini's by the Sea
Downtown Johnny
Elephant Bar
Eric's Ribs
Firehouse
Gathering
Hamburger Mary's
Hang Ten
Harbor House
Hard Rock Cafe
Hind Quarter
Hob Nob Hill
Hodad's
HomeTown Buffet
Hops Bistro
Ida Bailey's
Islands Fine Burgers
Jared's
Jimmy Carter's Cafe
Johnny Rockets
John's Waffle Shop
Karl Strauss Brew. Gardens
Karl Strauss Brew./Grill
Kenny's Steak Pub
Kono's Cafe
Lael's
La Valencia
Lobster Co.
Longhorn Cafe
Milligan's B&G
Mission Coffee Cup
Mission Hills Café
Montanas Grill
Morton's
Neiman's
94th Aero Squadron
Old Ox
Original Pancake Hse.
Oscar's
Pine Valley Hse.
Poseidon
Putnam's
Quails Inn
Rainwater's
Red Tracton's
Rimel's Rotisserie

Ruby's Diner
Ruth's Chris
San Diego Brewing
San Diego Chicken Pie
Screens Bistro
Soup Exchange
Souplantation
Spoons Grill & Bar
St. Germain's Cafe
T.G.I. Friday's
Tom Ham's Lighthse.
Trophy's
World Famous

Asian

Cafe Japengo
Chino
Kemo Sabe
Roppongi
Taka
Terra
Yen's Wok

Bakeries

Bread & Cie.
Come On In!
Girard Gourmet
Karen Krasne's

Bar-B-Q

Buffalo Joe's
Claim Jumper
Dick's Last Resort
Eric's Ribs
Fargo's BBQ
Hang Ten
Kansas City BBQ
Longhorn Cafe
Montanas Grill
Phil's Barbecue
Pine Hills Lodge
Tony Roma's

Belgian

Belgian Lion
Girard Gourmet

Cajun/Creole

Bayou B&G
Chateau Orleans
Gulf Coast Grill
Gumbo Pot
Maranto's Mardi Gras
Sherman's

Californian

Azzura Point
Baily Wine Country
Bellefleur Winery
Bird Rock Cafe
Bistro Yang
Cafe Champagne
Cafe Pacifica
Cafe 222
Cafe Zinc
California Bistro
California Cafe B&G
California Cuisine
California Pizza Kit.
Charlie's by the Sea
Chuey's
Come On In!
Cottage
Crocodile Cafe
Delicias
Dining Room
D'Lish Bistro
Fifth & Hawthorne
George's at the Cove
Grant Grill
Green Flash
Jake's
La Jolla Brewing
Lamont St. Grill
Le Fontainebleau
Newport Ave. B&G
Pacifica Del Mar
Pacific Coast Grill
Pamplemousse Grille
Paper Moon Cafe
Planet Hollywood
Qwiigs B&G
Rancho Valencia
Rhinoceros Cafe
Sammy's Pizza
San Diego Pier Cafe
Torreyana Grille
Tupelo
Wolfgang Puck Café

Caribbean

Andres Cuban
Fargo's BBQ
Parrot Grill

Chinese

Bistro Yang
China Camp
China Inn
Chu Dynasty

Emerald Chinese
Emperor's Palace
Fortune Cookie
Great Wall Cafe
Healthy Chinese
Hong Kong
Hsu's Szechuwan
Imperial Mandarin
Jasmine
Mandarin China
Mandarin Dynasty
Mandarin Garden
Mandarin House
Miss China
Panda Country
Panda Inn
Peking Palace
P.F. Chang's
Pick Up Stix
Sze Chuan
Tin Ching
Yen's Wok

Coffeehouses/Desserts

Karen Krasne's
Living Room

Coffee Shops/Diners

Big Kitchen
Cecil's Cafe
Corvette Diner
Crest Cafe
Harry's Coffee Shop
Hob Nob Hill
Jimmy Carter's Cafe
Johnny Rockets
Mission
Mission Coffee Cup
Ruby's Diner

Continental

Chez Loma
Crown Room
Imperial House
Inn at the Park
La Valencia
Mister A's
Rancho Valencia
Rest. Europa
St. James Bar
Top o' the Cove

Cuban

Andres Cuban

Delis/Sandwich Shops

Canora's
City Deli
D.Z. Akin's
Girard Gourmet
Hershel's
Milton's Deli
Samson's

Dim Sum

Emerald Chinese
Imperial Mandarin
Jasmine
Mandarin China
Mandarin Garden

Eclectic/International

D'Lish Bistro
Mission
Mixx
150 Grand Café
Parkhouse Eatery
Peter & Harry's
Taka
Torrey Pines Cafe

English

Princess Pub

Ethiopian

Asmara
Red Sea

Fondue

Forever Fondue

French

Belgian Lion
Cafe Eleven
El Bizcocho
French Gourmet
La Bonne Bouffe
Le Fontainebleau
Liaison
Maitre D'
Sirino's
Thee Bungalow

French Bistro

Bread & Cie.
French Gourmet
French Mkt. Grille
La Bonne Bouffe
La Provence
La Vache & Co.
La Valencia
Tapenade

French (New)
Bernard'O
Chez Loma
Cindy Black's
El Bizcocho
Grant Grill
Laurel
La Valencia
Marine Room
Mille Fleurs
Pamplemousse Grille
Vignola
WineSellar & Brasserie

German
House of Munich
Ingrid's
Kaiserhof
Karl Strauss Brew. Gardens
Karl Strauss Brew./Grill
Peter & Harry's
Rest. Europa

Greek
Aesop's Tables
Athens Market
Cafe Athena
Georgia's Greek
Greek Town

Hamburgers
Bully's
Corvette Diner
Downtown Johnny
Hamburger Mary's
Hard Rock Cafe
Hodad's
Islands Fine Burgers
Johnny Rockets
Karl Strauss Brew./Grill
La Jolla Brewing
Longhorn Cafe
Ruby's Diner
Seau's
Spoons Grill & Bar

Health Food
Daily's
Vegetarian Zone

Hungarian
Budapest Express

Indian
Ashoka Cuisine
Ashoka the Great

Bombay Exotic
Cafe India
KC's Tandoor
Maharajah
Star of India
World Curry

Indonesian
Bali Indonesian

Irish
Callahan's Pub
Field

Italian
(N=Northern; S=Southern;
N&S=Includes both)
Andiamo!! (N)
Arrivederci (N&S)
Asti Ristorante (N&S)
Baci (N&S)
Bell'agio (N&S)
Bella Luna (N&S)
Bollicine (N)
Busalacchi's (S)
Cafe Luna (N&S)
Cafe Zucchero (N&S)
Carino's (N&S)
De Luca's (N&S)
de Medici (N&S)
Embers Grille (N&S)
Filippi's Pizza (N&S)
Fio's Cucina (N)
Firenze Trattoria (N&S)
Il Fornaio (N&S)
Il Forno (N)
Italia Mia (N)
Itri (N&S)
Jack & Giulio's (N&S)
La Bruschetta (N&S)
Lader's (N&S)
La Scala (S)
La Taverna (N&S)
La Terrazza (N&S)
Lorna's (N&S)
Lotsa Pasta (N&S)
Manhattan (N&S)
Old Spaghetti (N&S)
Old Trieste (N)
Old Venice (S)
Olive Garden (N&S)
Osteria Panevino (N)
Papachino's (N&S)
Parioli Italian Bistro (N&S)
Pasta Pronto (N&S)
Piatti (N&S)

Pizza Bella (N&S)
Pizza Nova (N&S)
Pizzeria Uno (N&S)
Prego (N&S)
Primavera (N)
Rist. Michelangelo (N&S)
Roma Beach Caffe (N&S)
Salvatore's (N)
Sante (N&S)
Sardina's Italian (S)
Scalini (N)
Trattoria Acqua (N&S)
Trattoria Fantastica (N&S)
Trattoria La Strada (N)
Trattoria Mannino (N&S)
Trattoria Portobello (N)
Trattoria Positano (N&S)
Tutto Mare (N&S)
Valentino's (N)
Venetian Rest. (N&S)
Vesuvio Gourmet (N&S)
Via Italia Trattoria (N)
Vicino Mare (N&S)
Vigilucci's Pizzeria (N&S)
Vigilucci's Trattoria (N&S)
Vivace (N)
When in Rome (N&S)
Zagarella (N&S)

Jamaican
Fargo's BBQ

Japanese
Banzai Cantina
Benihana
Cafe Japengo
Chino
Dao Son
Ichiban
Jin Sang
Katzra
Kazumi Sushi
Kiyo's
Kobe Misono
Little Tokyo
Mr. Sushi
Noodle House
Onami
Samurai of Japan
Shien of Osaka
Sushi on the Rock
Sushi Ota
Tajima
Taka
World Curry
Yakitori II

Yen's Wok
Yoshino
Yummy Maki

Jewish
City Deli
D.Z. Akin's
Milton's Deli
Samson's

Korean
Korea House
Korean Seoul Hse.
Yen's Wok

Latin American
Berta's

Mediterranean
Aesop's Tables
Aladdin Med. Cafe
Azzura Point
Bellefleur Winery
Olé Madrid
Palomino Euro Bistro
Sally's
Trattoria Acqua
Zeena's

Mexican/Tex-Mex
Alfonso's
Amigos Seafood
Banzai Cantina
Blue Bird Cafe
Casa De Bandini
Casa de Pico
Casa Guadalajara
Casa Machado
Cerveceria Santa Fe
Chilango's
Chuey's
El Agave
El Fandango
El Indio Shop
El Ranchero
El Tecolote
El Torito
Fidel's
Fins
Guava Beach
Hernandez Hideaway
Jose's Courtroom
La Especial Norte
La Fonda
La Paloma
La Salsa

Las Olas
Mexican Village
Miguel's Cocina
Old Town Mexican
On the Border
Palenque
Picoso
Rancho El Nopal
Rubio's Baja Grill
Su Casa
Taco Auctioneer
Tony's Jacal

Middle Eastern

Aladdin Med. Cafe
Fairouz Cafe
Khatoon
Khyber Pass
Zeena's

Moroccan

Marrakesh
Zeena's

Native American

Kemo Sabe

Noodle Shops

Saffron Noodles

Pacific Rim

Cafe Japengo
Guava Beach
Pacifica Del Mar
Peohe's
Rancho Valencia

Persian

BANDAR
Khatoon
Sadaf

Peruvian

Machupicchu

Pizza

B.J.'s Pizza
Bronx Pizza
Cafe Zucchero
California Pizza Kit.
Carino's
D'Lish Bistro
Embers Grille
Filippi's Pizza
Il Forno
Italia Mia
Oscar's

Papachino's
Pizza Bella
Pizza Nova
Pizzeria Uno
Sammy's Pizza
Trophy's
Venetian Rest.
Via Italia Trattoria
Vigilucci's Pizzeria
Zeena's

Russian

Little Russia

Seafood

Amigos Seafood
Anthony's Fishette
Anthony's Fish Grotto
Anthony's Star
Beach House
Blue Crab
Blue Point Coastal
Boathouse
Brigantine
Cafe Pacifica
Cecil's Cafe
Cerveceria Santa Fe
Charlie's by the Sea
Chart House
Crab Catcher
de Medici
Dini's by the Sea
Fifth & Hawthorne
Fins
Fish House
Fish Market
Fish Merchant
Gulf Coast Grill
Harbor House
Hind Quarter
Jake's
Jared's
Jasmine
Joe's Crab Shack
La Mesa
La Valencia
Lobster Co.
Old Ox
Pacifica Del Mar
Pacific Coast Grill
Peohe's
Pisces
Point Loma Seafoods
Poseidon
Primavera
Qwiigs B&G

Reuben's
Rimel's Rotisserie
Rusty Pelican
Sally's
Sand Crab Cafe
San Diego Pier Cafe
Saska's
Shores
Sportsmen's Seafoods
Tapenade
TD Hays
Top of the Market
Tutto Mare
Vicino Mare
World Famous

Soup/Salad Bars
Soup Exchange
Souplantation

South American
Berta's

Southern/Soul
Gulf Coast Grill
Juke Joint Cafe
Sherman's

Southwestern
Cilantros
Coyote B&G
Croce's
Dakota Grill
Epazote
Kemo Sabe

Spanish
La Gran Tapa
Olé Madrid
Sevilla

Steakhouses
Albie's Beef Inn
Bully's
Butcher Shop
Cafe La Maze
Chart House
Eric's Ribs
Harbor House
Hind Quarter

Jared's
Kenny's Steak Pub
La Valencia
Milligan's B&G
Morton's
Old Ox
Outback Steakhse.
Pinnacle Peak
Rainwater's
Red Tracton's
Reuben's
Ruth's Chris
Saska's
Stuart Anderson's
TD Hays

Thai
Bai Yook
Bangkok Thai
Celadon
Di-Chan
Karinya
Royal Thai Cuisine
Saffron Chicken
Saffron Noodles
Siam
Spice & Rice
Spices Thai Cafe
Swadee Thai
Taste of Thai
Thaigo
Thai House
Thai Orchid
World Curry

Vegetarian
(Most Chinese, Indian and
Thai restaurants)
Cafe Zinc
Jyoti-Bihanga
Vegetarian Zone

Vietnamese
A-Dong
Dao Son
Le Bambou
Pho Pasteur
Phuong Trang

LOCATIONS

Beaches/Coastal

Bangkok Thai
Beach House
Belgian Lion
Bellefleur Winery
Blue Bird Cafe
Blue Crab
Boathouse
Brigantine
Budapest Express
Bully's
Cafe Athena
Cafe Zinc
California Bistro
California Pizza Kit.
Cass Street B&G
Cecil's Cafe
Charlie's by the Sea
Chart House
Chateau Orleans
China Inn
Cilantros
Claim Jumper
Coyote B&G
Dining Room
Dini's by the Sea
El Torito
Epazote
Fidel's
Filippi's Pizza
Firehouse
Firenze Trattoria
Fish House
Fish Market
French Gourmet
Green Flash
Guava Beach
Hershel's
Hodad's
HomeTown Buffet
Humphrey's
Il Fornaio
Ingrid's
Jake's
Jared's
Johnny Rockets
Kaiserhof
Karinya
Kono's Cafe
La Bonne Bouffe
La Especial Norte
Lamont St. Grill

La Salsa
Las Olas
Le Bambou
Lotsa Pasta
Machupicchu
Maranto's Mardi Gras
Miguel's Cocina
Milton's Deli
Mission
Mr. Sushi
Neiman's
Newport Ave. B&G
Old Ox
Old Venice
Original Pancake Hse.
Oscar's
Pacifica Del Mar
Pacific Coast Grill
Palenque
Pamplemousse Grille
Papachino's
Parioli Italian Bistro
Pasta Pronto
Peter & Harry's
Pick Up Stix
Pisces
Pizza Nova
Pizzeria Uno
Point Loma Seafoods
Poseidon
Qwiigs B&G
Red Tracton's
Rist. Michelangelo
Rubio's Baja Grill
Ruby's Diner
Rusty Pelican
Sammy's Pizza
Samurai of Japan
Saska's
Sbicca
Scalini
Soup Exchange
Souplantation
Spices Thai Cafe
Spoons Grill & Bar
Sportsmen's Seafoods
St. Germain's Cafe
Stuart Anderson's
Sushi Ota
Taco Auctioneer
Taste of Thai
TD Hays
Thee Bungalow

Tin Ching
Tom Ham's Lighthse.
Tony Roma's
Tony's Jacal
Torrey Pines Cafe
Trattoria Positano
Venetian Rest.
Vigilucci's Pizzeria
Vigilucci's Trattoria
Vivace
When in Rome
World Curry
World Famous

Coronado
Azzura Point
Brigantine
Chart House
Chez Loma
Chu Dynasty
Crown Room
La Salsa
L'Escale
Market Cafe
Mexican Village
Miguel's Cocina
Peohe's
Primavera
Prince of Wales
Rhinoceros Cafe
Swadee Thai

Downtown
Anthony's Fishette
Anthony's Fish Grotto
Anthony's Star
Athens Market
Cafe 222
Cafe Zucchero
California Cafe B&G
Cerveceria Santa Fe
Chart House
China Camp
Dobson's
Downtown Johnny
Filippi's Pizza
Fish Market
Grant Grill
Harbor House
Hob Nob Hill
Imperial House
Kansas City BBQ
Karl Strauss Brew./Grill
Lael's
La Gran Tapa
La Salsa

Laurel
Le Fontainebleau
Liaison
Mandarin House
Mister A's
Morton's
Panda Inn
Planet Hollywood
Princess Pub
Rainwater's
Rubio's Baja Grill
Ruth's Chris
Sally's
Salvatore's
San Diego Pier Cafe
Top of the Market
Trattoria Fantastica
Vicino Mare
Zagarella

East County
Anthony's Fish Grotto
Brigantine
Claim Jumper
D.Z. Akin's
El Torito
HomeTown Buffet
Lader's
La Mesa
La Salsa
Little Russia
Olive Garden
Oscar's
Outback Steakhse.
Panda Country
Papachino's
Pick Up Stix
Pine Hills Lodge
Pine Valley Hse.
Pinnacle Peak
Pizza Nova
Sherman's
Souplantation
Stuart Anderson's
Trophy's

Gaslamp
Asti Ristorante
BANDAR
Bayou B&G
Bella Luna
Blue Point Coastal
Buffalo Joe's
Chino
Croce's
Dakota Grill

de Medici
Dick's Last Resort
El Indio Shop
Field
Fio's Cucina
Greek Town
Hang Ten
Hard Rock Cafe
Ida Bailey's
Itri
Juke Joint Cafe
Kenny's Steak Pub
Kiyo's
La Provence
Lobster Co.
Old Spaghetti
Olé Madrid
Osteria Panevino
Paper Moon Cafe
Parrot Grill
Royal Thai Cuisine
Rubio's Baja Grill
Sadaf
Sammy's Pizza
Sevilla
Star of India
Taka
Trattoria La Strada
Trattoria Portobello
Tupelo
Vignola
Zeena's

La Jolla/Golden Triangle
Aesop's Tables
Alfonso's
Ashoka Cuisine
Bali Indonesian
Bird Rock Cafe
B.J.'s Pizza
Bollicine
Brockton Villa
Bully's
Cafe Japengo
California Pizza Kit.
Carino's
Chart House
Cindy Black's
Cody's
Come On In!
Cottage
Crab Catcher
Crescent Shores
Daily's
D'Lish Bistro

El Ranchero
El Torito
Fins
Forever Fondue
George's at the Cove
Girard Gourmet
Hard Rock Cafe
Harry's Coffee Shop
Healthy Chinese
Hops Bistro
Il Forno
Islands Fine Burgers
Jin Sang
John's Waffle Shop
Jose's Courtroom
Karl Strauss Brew. Gardens
Karl Strauss Brew./Grill
KC's Tandoor
Khatoon
La Bruschetta
La Fonda
La Jolla Brewing
La Salsa
La Taverna
La Terrazza
La Valencia
Living Room
Lorna's
Maitre D'
Mandarin House
Manhattan
Marine Room
Marrakesh
Milligan's B&G
Miss China
Mission Coffee Cup
Palomino Euro Bistro
Panda Country
Papachino's
Peking Palace
P.F. Chang's
Piatti
Pick Up Stix
Picoso
Putnam's
Rimel's Rotisserie
Roma Beach Caffe
Roppongi
Royal Thai Cuisine
Rubio's Baja Grill
Sadaf
Sammy's Pizza
Samson's
Sante
Shores

Spice & Rice
Star of India
St. James Bar
Su Casa
Sushi on the Rock
Tapenade
T.G.I. Friday's
Top o' the Cove
Torreyana Grille
Trattoria Acqua
Trattoria Mannino
Trophy's
Tutto Mare
Yen's Wok
Yummy Maki

Mission Valley

Adam's Steak & Eggs
Albie's Beef Inn
Benihana
Bennigan's
Bully's
Crocodile Cafe
El Tecolote
El Torito
Fins
Joe's Crab Shack
KC's Tandoor
On the Border
Oscar's
Peking Palace
Pizzeria Uno
Postcards
Prego
Rubio's Baja Grill
Ruby's Diner
Sammy's Pizza
Screens Bistro
Seau's
T.G.I. Friday's
Trophy's
Wolfgang Puck Café

North County

Anthony's Fish Grotto
Bernard'O
Brigantine
Cafe Luna
California Pizza Kit.
Claim Jumper
Delicias
El Bizcocho
Elephant Bar
El Torito
Emperor's Palace
Filippi's Pizza

Fins
Fish House
Fortune Cookie
French Mkt. Grille
Gumbo Pot
Hernandez Hideaway
HomeTown Buffet
Islands Fine Burgers
Italia Mia
La Paloma
La Salsa
Little Tokyo
Mille Fleurs
Old Spaghetti
Olive Garden
Onami
150 Grand Café
Original Pancake Hse.
Oscar's
Outback Steakhse.
Papachino's
Pick Up Stix
Quails Inn
Rancho Valencia
Sand Crab Cafe
Shien of Osaka
Sirino's
Souplantation
Spices Thai Cafe
Star of India
T.G.I. Friday's
Thaigo
Tony Roma's
Valentino's

Old Town

Amigos Seafood
Berta's
Brigantine
Cafe Pacifica
Casa De Bandini
Casa de Pico
Casa Guadalajara
El Agave
El Fandango
Eric's Ribs
Great Wall Cafe
Jack & Giulio's
Old Town Mexican
Pizza Bella
Rancho El Nopal

San Diego

A-Dong
Aladdin Med. Cafe
Andiamo!!

Andres Cuban
Ashoka the Great
Asmara
Baci
Banzai Cantina
Bell'agio
Big Kitchen
Bistro Yang
Butcher Shop
Cafe India
Callahan's Pub
Canora's
Casa Machado
Chuey's
Dao Son
Di-Chan
El Indio Shop
El Torito
Embers Grille
Emerald Chinese
Fairouz Cafe
Fargo's BBQ
Fifth & Hawthorne
Filippi's Pizza
Fins
Fish Merchant
Georgia's Greek
Healthy Chinese
Hind Quarter
HomeTown Buffet
Hsu's Szechuwan
Imperial Mandarin
Islands Fine Burgers
Jasmine
Jyoti-Bihanga
Kabul West
Katzra
Kensington Grill
Khyber Pass
Kobe Misono
Korea House
La Salsa
La Scala
Living Room
Longhorn Cafe
Mandarin China
Mandarin Garden
Mission
94th Aero Squadron
Noodle House
Old Trieste
Olive Garden
Original Pancake Hse.
Outback Steakhse.
Panda Country

Pho Pasteur
Phuong Trang
Red Sea
Rest. Europa
Rubio's Baja Grill
Saffron Chicken
Saffron Noodles
San Diego Brewing
Sardina's Italian
Siam
Soup Exchange
Souplantation
Stuart Anderson's
Sze Chuan
Tajima
Thai House
Thai Orchid
Tony Roma's
Vesuvio Gourmet
Via Italia Trattoria
WineSellar & Brasserie
Yakitori II
Yoshino

South Bay
Anthony's Fish Grotto
Butcher Shop
Cafe La Maze
D'Lish Bistro
El Torito
HomeTown Buffet
House of Munich
Jake's
Olive Garden
Soup Exchange
Stuart Anderson's

Temecula
Baily Wine Country
Cafe Champagne

Uptown/Hillcrest
Adam's Ave. Grill
Arrivederci
Bai Yook
Bombay Exotic
Bread & Cie.
Bronx Pizza
Busalacchi's
Cafe Eleven
Cafe on Park
California Cuisine
Celadon
Chilango's
City Deli
Corvette Diner

Crest Cafe
De Luca's
Gathering
Gulf Coast Grill
Hamburger Mary's
Hong Kong
Ichiban
Inn at the Park
Jimmy Carter's Cafe
Karen Krasne's
Kazumi Sushi
Kemo Sabe
Korean Seoul Hse.
La Salsa
La Vache & Co.
Living Room

Maharajah
Mandarin Dynasty
Mission Hills Café
Mixx
Montanas Grill
Parkhouse Eatery
Pasta Pronto
Phil's Barbecue
Pick Up Stix
Pizza Nova
Rubio's Baja Grill
San Diego Chicken Pie
Taste of Thai
Terra
Vegetarian Zone

SPECIAL FEATURES AND APPEALS

Breakfast

(All hotels and the following standouts)

Adam's Steak & Eggs
Big Kitchen
Brockton Villa
Cafe 222
Cafe Zinc
Canora's
Cecil's Cafe
City Deli
Cody's
Come On In!
Cottage
Crest Cafe
El Indio Shop
Field
Firehouse
French Gourmet
Gathering
Green Flash
Hamburger Mary's
Hob Nob Hill
Il Fornaio
Ingrid's
Jimmy Carter's Cafe
John's Waffle Shop
Jyoti-Bihanga
Kono's Cafe
Living Room
Longhorn Cafe
Milton's Deli
Mission
Mission Coffee Cup
Mission Hills Café
Original Pancake Hse.
Princess Pub
Rancho El Nopal
Ruby's Diner
Samson's
San Diego Pier Cafe
St. Germain's Cafe

Buffet Served

(Check prices, days and times)

Ashoka the Great
BANDAR
Banzai Cantina
Bombay Exotic
Cafe India
Chu Dynasty

Crown Room
De Luca's
El Bizcocho
Fairouz Cafe
Hamburger Mary's
Ida Bailey's
Inn at the Park
Jake's
Karl Strauss Brew. Gardens
KC's Tandoor
Khyber Pass
Kono's Cafe
Lael's
Le Fontainebleau
Living Room
Marine Room
Market Cafe
94th Aero Squadron
Pine Hills Lodge
Quails Inn
Rusty Pelican
Sherman's
Shores
Soup Exchange
Souplantation
Star of India
Tom Ham's Lighthse.
Torreyana Grille

Business Dining

Anthony's Star
Asti Ristorante
Athens Market
Azzura Point
Baci
Bellefleur Winery
Bernard'O
Blue Point Coastal
Cafe Champagne
Cafe Japengo
Cafe Pacifica
Chart House
Crescent Shores
Crown Room
Delicias
Dining Room
Dobson's
El Bizcocho
Fifth & Hawthorne
Firenze Trattoria
Grant Grill
Hob Nob Hill
Jake's

Jared's
Kobe Misono
Korea House
La Gran Tapa
Laurel
La Valencia
Le Fontainebleau
Maitre D'
Manhattan
Marine Room
Mille Fleurs
Mister A's
Morton's
150 Grand Café
Pamplemousse Grille
Panda Country
P.F. Chang's
Pisces
Primavera
Prince of Wales
Rainwater's
Rancho Valencia
Red Tracton's
Ruth's Chris
Sally's
Salvatore's
Sante
Shores
St. James Bar
Taka
TD Hays
Thee Bungalow
Tom Ham's Lighthse.
Top of the Market
Top o' the Cove
Trattoria Acqua
Trattoria Positano
Tutto Mare
Valentino's
Vivace
When in Rome
WineSellar & Brasserie

Caters
(Best of many)
A-Dong
Aesop's Tables
Andiamo!!
Arrivederci
Ashoka the Great
Athens Market
Baily Wine Country
BANDAR
Bayou B&G
Big Kitchen

Bird Rock Cafe
Blue Point Coastal
Bombay Exotic
Busalacchi's
Cafe on Park
Cafe Zucchero
California Cuisine
Chilango's
Chuey's
Cilantros
Cindy Black's
Delicias
D.Z. Akin's
El Agave
El Indio Shop
Embers Grille
Epazote
Fargo's BBQ
French Mkt. Grille
Grant Grill
Il Forno
Ingrid's
Itri
Karen Krasne's
Karinya
KC's Tandoor
Kemo Sabe
Khyber Pass
La Fonda
La Salsa
La Scala
Las Olas
La Terrazza
Lorna's
Lotsa Pasta
Mission
Mission Coffee Cup
Mission Hills Café
Mixx
Old Town Mexican
150 Grand Café
Oscar's
Osteria Panevino
Pacifica Del Mar
Pacific Coast Grill
Pamplemousse Grille
Parioli Italian Bistro
Parkhouse Eatery
Piatti
Rancho Valencia
Rist. Michelangelo
Royal Thai Cuisine
Sally's
Sammy's Pizza
Scalini

116

Sevilla
Sirino's
Spice & Rice
Sushi on the Rock
Tapenade
Tony's Jacal
Trattoria Fantastica
Trattoria Mannino
Trattoria Portobello
Tutto Mare
Vesuvio Gourmet
Vicino Mare
Vigilucci's Pizzeria
Vigilucci's Trattoria
Vignola
When in Rome
Yen's Wok

Cigar Friendly

Blue Point Coastal
Cafe Champagne
Cilantros
Epazote
Il Fornaio
Il Forno
Jared's
Kensington Grill
La Valencia
Osteria Panevino
Pacific Coast Grill
Parioli Italian Bistro
Parkhouse Eatery
Piatti
Point Loma Seafoods
Princess Pub
Putnam's
Rest. Europa
Sally's
Sammy's Pizza
Sante
Seau's
Top o' the Cove
Trattoria Acqua
Trattoria Portobello
Trophy's
Tutto Mare
Vigilucci's Pizzeria
Vignola

Dancing/Entertainment

(Check days, times and
performers for entertainment;
D=dancing; best of many)
Albie's Beef Inn (piano)
Azzura Point (piano)

Bayou B&G (piano)
Beach House (jazz)
Bellefleur Winery (jazz)
Buffalo Joe's (D/varies)
California Cafe B&G (Latin jazz)
Callahan's Pub (Irish)
Casa De Bandini (mariachi)
Casa Guadalajara (D/mariachi)
Chateau Orleans (blues)
Chino (D)
Chuey's (bands)
Coyote B&G (D)
Crescent Shores (jazz)
Croce's (jazz/R&B)
Crown Room (piano)
Dakota Grill (piano)
Delicias (guitar)
Dick's Last Resort (bands)
El Bizcocho (piano)
Epazote (D/jazz)
Fio's Cucina (piano)
Gathering (jazz/magic)
Grant Grill (blues/jazz)
Hamburger Mary's (D)
Hind Quarter (karaoke)
House of Munich (accordion)
Humphrey's (varies)
Ida Bailey's (piano)
Il Forno (varies)
Imperial House (D/piano)
Ingrid's (varies)
Inn at the Park (piano/vocals)
Joe's Crab Shack (D)
Juke Joint Cafe (jazz)
Karl Strauss Brew. Gardens
   (jazz)
Kenny's Steak Pub (piano)
Laurel (guitar/piano)
Le Fontainebleau (piano)
Little Russia (D/Russian)
Lotsa Pasta (jazz)
Maitre D' (piano)
Marine Room (D)
Marrakesh (belly dancer)
Mille Fleurs (piano)
Milligan's B&G (blues/jazz)
Mixx (blues/jazz)
Mister A's (piano)
Neiman's (D/swing)
94th Aero Squadron (D)
Old Town Mexican (mariachi)
Old Venice (blues/jazz)
Olé Madrid (D/flamenco/jazz)
Pine Hills Lodge (dinner theater)
Prince of Wales (jazz/piano)

Princess Pub (piano)
Quails Inn (D/piano)
Rancho El Nopal
    (mariachi/Peruvian)
Rancho Valencia (guitar)
Red Tracton's (piano)
Rest. Europa (piano)
Roma Beach Caffe (piano)
Sally's (jazz)
Samson's (violin)
Sante (piano)
Scalini (piano)
Seau's (jazz/R&B)
Sherman's (jazz)
Stuart Anderson's (varies)
Tom Ham's Lighthse. (piano)
Torreyana Grille (D/jazz)
Trattoria Mannino (blues/jazz)
Tutto Mare (jazz)

Delivers*/Takeout

(Nearly all Asians, coffee
shops, delis, diners and
pasta/pizzerias deliver or do
takeout; here are some
interesting possibilities;
D=delivery, T=takeout; *call
to check range and charges,
if any)
Aesop's Tables (D,T)
Aladdin Med. Cafe (T)
Albie's Beef Inn (T)
Alfonso's (T)
Andiamo!! (T)
Andres Cuban (D,T)
Anthony's Fish Grotto (T)
Arrivederci (T)
Ashoka Cuisine (D)
Asmara (T)
Athens Market (D,T)
Baci (D,T)
Baily Wine Country (T)
Bali Indonesian (T)
BANDAR(D,T)
Bayou B&G (T)
Bell'agio (T)
Bellefleur Winery (T)
Berta's (T)
Bird Rock Cafe (D,T)
Blue Bird Cafe (T)
Blue Point Coastal (T)
Boathouse (T)
Bollicine (T)
Bombay Exotic (T)
Buffalo Joe's (D,T)

Bully's (T)
Busalacchi's (T)
Cafe Eleven (T)
Cafe India (D,T)
Cafe on Park (T)
Cafe Pacifica (T)
California Cuisine (T)
Canora's India St. (T)
Casa De Bandini (T)
Casa Guadalajara (T)
Casa Machado (T)
Cecil's Cafe (T)
Cerveceria Santa Fe (T)
Chateau Orleans (T)
Chez Loma (T)
Chilango's (D,T)
Cilantros (T)
Cindy Black's (T)
Cottage (D,T)
Crab Catcher (T)
Crocodile Cafe (T)
Dakota Grill (T)
Delicias (T)
de Medici (T)
Dining Room (T)
Dini's by the Sea (T)
Epazote (T)
Eric's Ribs (T)
Fairouz Cafe (D,T)
Fargo's BBQ (T)
Fidel's (T)
Field (T)
Firenze Trattoria (D,T)
Fish House (T)
Fish Market (T)
Fish Merchant (T)
French Gourmet (T)
French Mkt. Grille (T)
Gathering (T)
Georgia's Greek (T)
Hang Ten (T)
Hard Rock Cafe (T)
Hind Quarter (T)
Hodad's (T)
Hops Bistro (T)
House of Munich (T)
Ida Bailey's (T)
Il Fornaio (T)
Il Forno (D,T)
Ingrid's (T)
Italia Mia (T)
Itri (T)
Jack & Giulio's (T)
Jake's (T)
Jimmy Carter's Cafe (T)

Joe's Crab Shack (T)
Jose's Courtroom (T)
Juke Joint Cafe (T)
Jyoti-Bihanga (T)
Kabul West (D,T)
Kaiserhof (T)
Kansas City BBQ (T)
Karl Strauss Brew. Gardens (D,T)
Karl Strauss Brew./Grill (T)
KC's Tandoor (D,T)
Kenny's Steak Pub (T)
Kensington Grill (T)
Khatoon (T)
Khyber Pass (T)
Kono's Cafe (T)
La Bruschetta (T)
Lael's (T)
La Fonda (T)
La Mesa (T)
Lamont St. Grill (T)
La Scala (T)
Las Olas (T)
La Terrazza (T)
La Vache & Co. (D,T)
Liaison (T)
Little Russia (T)
Longhorn Cafe (T)
Lorna's (D,T)
Machupicchu (T)
Maharajah (T)
Manhattan (T)
Market Cafe (T)
Marrakesh (T)
Mexican Village (T)
Milligan's B&G (T)
Mixx (T)
Montanas Grill (D,T)
Neiman's (T)
Newport Ave. B&G (T)
Old Ox (T)
150 Grand Café (T)
Osteria Panevino (T)
Pacifica Del Mar (T)
Pacific Coast Grill (T)
Palenque (T)
Pamplemousse Grille (T)
Parioli Italian Bistro (T)
Parrot Grill (T)
Piatti (T)
Picoso (D,T)
Pine Valley Hse. (T)
Pinnacle Peak (T)
Point Loma Seafoods (T)
Postcards (T)

Princess Pub (T)
Quails Inn (T)
Qwiigs B&G (T)
Rainwater's (T)
Rancho Valencia (T)
Red Sea (T)
Red Tracton's (T)
Rest. Europa (D,T)
Rhinoceros Cafe (D,T)
Rimel's Rotisserie (T)
Rist. Michelangelo (T)
Ruth's Chris (T)
Sally's (T)
Salvatore's (T)
Sand Crab Cafe (T)
San Diego Brewing (T)
San Diego Chicken Pie (T)
Scalini (T)
Seau's (T)
Sportsmen's Seafoods (T)
St. Germain's Cafe (T)
St. James Bar (T)
Stuart Anderson's (T)
Su Casa (D,T)
TD Hays (D)
Terra (T)
Tony's Jacal (T)
Torreyana Grille (D,T)
Torrey Pines Cafe (T)
Trattoria Acqua (T)
Trattoria Mannino (D,T)
Trattoria Portobello (T)
Trattoria Positano (T)
Trophy's (T)
Tupelo (T)
Tutto Mare (D,T)
Vegetarian Zone (T)
Vesuvio Gourmet (D,T)
Vicino Mare (T)
Vignola (T)
When in Rome (T)
Wolfgang Puck Café (T)
World Famous (T)
Zagarella (T)

Dining Alone

(Other than hotels, coffee shops, sushi bars and places with counter service)

Asti Ristorante
Bernard'O
Chilango's
Daily's
Dobson's
D.Z. Akin's

119

El Indio Shop
Jasmine
Karen Krasne's
Laurel
L'Escale
Panda Country
Pizza Nova
Rainwater's
Salvatore's
Sammy's Pizza
Samson's
Sante
Soup Exchange
Souplantation
Top of the Market
Top o' the Cove
Trattoria Mannino
Trattoria Positano
When in Rome

Fireplaces

Aesop's Tables
Albie's Beef Inn
Brockton Villa
Busalacchi's
Chart House
Chu Dynasty
Claim Jumper
Delicias
Dining Room
El Bizcocho
El Fandango
Epazote
Fish Market
Great Wall Cafe
Guava Beach
Kaiserhof
Lamont St. Grill
La Valencia
Mille Fleurs
Milligan's B&G
Neiman's
94th Aero Squadron
150 Grand Café
Parkhouse Eatery
Poseidon
Princess Pub
Rancho Valencia
Sante
Sbicca
Su Casa
Thee Bungalow
Top o' the Cove
Vivace

Health/Spa Menus

(Most places cook to order to
meet any dietary request;
call in advance to check;
almost all Chinese, Indian and
other ethnics have
health-conscious
meals, as do the following)
Arrivederci
Bayou B&G
Buffalo Joe's
Cafe India
Cafe Zinc
California Bistro
Casa De Bandini
Daily's
Lotsa Pasta
Mission Coffee Cup
Pisces
Rancho Valencia
Vegetarian Zone
Vivace

Historic Interest

(Year opened; *building)
1886 Neiman's*
1887 Chart House*
1888 Crown Room*
1894 Brockton Villa*
1905 BANDAR*
1910 Grant Grill*
1911 Bayou B&G*
1926 La Valencia*
1927 Pine Valley Hse.
1928 Putnam's
1938 San Diego Chicken Pie
1939 El Ranchero
1940 Carino's
1940 El Indio Shop
1940 Marine Room
1944 Hob Nob Hill
1945 Mexican Village
1946 Anthony's Fish Grotto
1946 Tony's Jacal
1951 Saska's

Hotel Dining

Colonial Inn
  Putnam's
Coronado Island Marriott
  L'Escale
Empress Hotel
  Manhattan

Four Seasons Resort Aviara
  California Bistro
  Vivace
Handlery Hotel
  Postcards
Hilton La Jolla Torrey Pines
  Torreyana Grille
Horton Grand Hotel
  Ida Bailey's
Hotel del Coronado
  Crown Room
  Prince of Wales
Hotel La Jolla
  Crescent Shores
Humphrey's Half Moon Inn
  Humphrey's
Hyatt Regency Hotel
  Lael's
  Sally's
La Costa Resort & Spa
  Pisces
L'Auberge Del Mar
  Dining Room
La Valencia
  La Valencia
Loews Coronado Bay Resort
  Azzura Point
  Market Cafe
Park Manor Suites
  Inn at the Park
Pine Hills Lodge
  Pine Hills Lodge
Rancho Bernardo Inn
  El Bizcocho
Rancho Valencia Resort
  Rancho Valencia
Sea Lodge Hotel
  Shores
St. James Hotel
  Vignola
Tamarack Beach Resort
  Dini's by the Sea
Travelodge
  Adam's Steak & Eggs
  Albie's Beef Inn
U.S. Grant Hotel
  Grant Grill
Westgate Hotel
  Le Fontainebleau

"In" Places
Anthony's Star
Azzura Point
Belgian Lion
Bellefleur Winery

Bird Rock Cafe
Blue Point Coastal
Bread & Cie.
Bully's
Cafe Eleven
Cafe Japengo
Cafe Pacifica
California Cuisine
Chez Loma
Delicias
Dobson's
El Bizcocho
Emerald Chinese
Fio's Cucina
George's at the Cove
Hard Rock Cafe
Hob Nob Hill
Jake's
Jasmine
Joe's Crab Shack
Karen Krasne's
La Bonne Bouffe
Laurel
Manhattan
Marine Room
Mexican Village
Mille Fleurs
Mister A's
Morton's
Old Ox
150 Grand Café
Osteria Panevino
Pacifica Del Mar
Pamplemousse Grille
Panda Inn
Parioli Italian Bistro
Peohe's
P.F. Chang's
Piatti
Prego
Primavera
Rancho Valencia
Roppongi
Ruth's Chris
Sante
Scalini
Sushi on the Rock
Sushi Ota
Tapenade
Top o' the Cove
Trattoria Acqua
Trattoria La Strada
Vivace
WineSellar & Brasserie

Jacket Required

Azzura Point
Dining Room
El Bizcocho
La Valencia
Le Fontainebleau
Little Russia
Mister A's
Old Trieste
Pisces

Late Late – After 12:30

(All hours are AM)
Bennigan's (1)
Hong Kong (3)
Kansas City BBQ (1)
Living Room (1)
Milligan's B&G (1:30)
Pizzeria Uno (2)
Saska's (2)
T.G.I. Friday's (1:30)

Meet for a Drink

(Most top hotels and the
following standouts)
Alfonso's
Athens Market
Bayou B&G
Bellefleur Winery
Bennigan's
Blue Point Coastal
Brigantine
Bully's
Callahan's Pub
Cerveceria Santa Fe
Chart House
Chino
Cilantros
Coyote B&G
Croce's
Dick's Last Resort
Downtown Johnny
Elephant Bar
El Torito
Epazote
Field
Green Flash
Hang Ten
Hard Rock Cafe
Kaiserhof
Karl Strauss Brew. Gardens
Karl Strauss Brew./Grill
Kenny's Steak Pub
Laurel
La Valencia

Marine Room
Milligan's B&G
Mister A's
Montanas Grill
Neiman's
Old Ox
Olé Madrid
150 Grand Café
Pacific Coast Grill
Palomino Euro Bistro
Pamplemousse Grille
Prego
Princess Pub
Rainwater's
Red Tracton's
Roppongi
Rusty Pelican
San Diego Brewing
Sante
Saska's
Scalini
Seau's
TD Hays
Tony Roma's
Top o' the Cove
Trophy's
Tutto Mare
When in Rome

Noteworthy Newcomers (29)

Bellefleur Winery
Bistro Yang
El Agave
Field
Forever Fondue
French Mkt. Grille
Gulf Coast Grill
Hang Ten
Jared's
Jin Sang
Juke Joint Cafe
La Bruschetta
La Fonda
La Vache & Co.
Lobster Co.
Mixx
Morton's
Palomino Euro Bistro
Pamplemousse Grille
Parioli Italian Bistro
Roma Beach Caffe
Roppongi
St. James Bar
Tapenade

Torrey Pines Cafe
Trattoria Positano
Vicino Mare
Vignola
Vivace

Noteworthy Closings (13)

Alize
Avanti
Bessie's Garret
Bistro Bacco
Brendory's by the Sea
Cha Cha Cha
Chung King Loh
Dansk Restaurant
Indigo Grill
Pachanga
Savoy
Sfuzzi
Toscas

Offbeat

Amigos Seafood
Banzai Cantina
Bayou B&G
Berta's
Blue Bird Cafe
Buffalo Joe's
Chilango's
Crest Cafe
Dick's Last Resort
Downtown Johnny
Fargo's BBQ
Green Flash
Guava Beach
Jyoti-Bihanga
Kemo Sabe
Kono's Cafe
Marrakesh
Mission
Mixx
Roppongi
Saska's
Sportsmen's Seafoods
Sushi on the Rock
Taco Auctioneer

Outdoor Dining

(G=garden; P=patio;
S=sidewalk; T=terrace;
W=waterside; best of many)
Aladdin Med. Cafe (P)
Alfonso's (P)
Ashoka Cuisine (P)
Asti Ristorante (P)
Baily Wine Country (P)

BANDAR (P)
Bayou B&G (P,S)
Beach House (P)
Bella Luna (S)
Bellefleur Winery (P)
Bird Rock Cafe (P,S,T)
Bistro Yang (P)
Blue Point Coastal (P)
Bombay Exotic (P)
Brockton Villa (P,T,W)
Busalacchi's (P)
Cafe Champagne (P)
Cafe Pacifica (P)
Cafe 222 (S)
Cafe Zinc (P)
Cafe Zucchero (P,S)
California Cafe B&G (P)
California Cuisine (G,P)
Casa de Pico (P)
Casa Guadalajara (P)
Cerveceria Santa Fe (P)
Charlie's by the Sea (P,W)
Chart House (P,W)
Chez Loma (S,T)
Cilantros (P)
Cottage (G)
Croce's (P,S)
Delicias (G,P)
de Medici (P)
Dini's by the Sea (P)
Downtown Johnny (P)
El Agave (P)
El Fandango (P)
El Indio Shop (P,S)
Epazote (P,T,W)
Fidel's (P)
Field (P)
Fio's Cucina (P)
Firehouse (T)
Fish Market (P,T,W)
French Mkt. Grille (P)
George's at the Cove (T,W)
Georgia's Greek (P)
Great Wall Cafe (P)
Green Flash (P,S,W)
Hamburger Mary's (G,P)
Hard Rock Cafe (P,S)
Humphrey's (W)
Il Fornaio (P,T)
Itri (P)
Jake's (P,W)
Johnny Rockets (P)
Kansas City BBQ (P)
Karen Krasne's (P)
Kensington Grill (S)

Kono's Cafe (P)
La Bruschetta (P)
Lael's (P)
Lamont St. Grill (P)
La Provence (P)
La Scala (P)
La Terrazza (T)
La Valencia (G,T)
L'Escale (P)
Lobster Co. (P)
Lotsa Pasta (P)
Marine Room (W)
Miguel's Cocina (P)
Mille Fleurs (P)
Mission Coffee Cup (P)
Mission Hills Café (G,S)
Old Venice (P)
Olé Madrid (P)
Osteria Panevino (P)
Pacifica Del Mar (T)
Palomino Euro Bistro (P)
Panda Inn (P)
Paper Moon Cafe (P,S)
Peohe's (P,T,W)
Piatti (G,P)
Picoso (P)
Point Loma Seafoods (P,S,W)
Poseidon (P,W)
Prego (P)
Putnam's (P,S,T)
Rainwater's (P)
Rancho El Nopal (P)
Rancho Valencia (P,T)
Rhinoceros Cafe (G,P,S)
Rimel's Rotisserie (P)
Royal Thai Cuisine (S)
Ruby's Diner (P,W)
Ruth's Chris (P)
Saffron Chicken (P)
Saffron Noodles (P)
Sally's (P,W)
Sammy's Pizza (G,P,S,T)
Sante (G,P)
Saska's (P)
Scalini (P)
Shores (P)
Sirino's (S)
Spice & Rice (G,P,S)
Star of India (P)
Su Casa (P)
Swadee Thai (P,T)
Taco Auctioneer (P)
Taka (P)
Tapenade (P,T)
Thee Bungalow (P)

Tony Roma's (P)
Top of the Market (W)
Top o' the Cove (P,T,W)
Torrey Pines Cafe (P)
Trattoria Acqua (G,W)
Trattoria Fantastica (P,S)
Trattoria La Strada (P)
Trattoria Mannino (P)
Trattoria Portobello (P)
Tutto Mare (P)
Vesuvio Gourmet (S)
Vicino Mare (P,S)
Vigilucci's Pizzeria (G,P)
Vignola (S,T)
Vivace (T)
When in Rome (G,P)
World Famous (P)

Outstanding Views

Anthony's Fishette
Anthony's Star
Ashoka Cuisine
Azzura Point
Beach House
Blue Crab
Boathouse
Bollicine
Brockton Villa
Cecil's Cafe
Charlie's by the Sea
Chart House
Crab Catcher
Crescent Shores
Dini's by the Sea
Edgewater Grill
El Agave
Epazote
Firehouse
Forever Fondue
George's at the Cove
Green Flash
Harbor House
Humphrey's
Il Fornaio
Jake's
Jared's
Kono's Cafe
La Terrazza
La Valencia
L'Escale
Marine Room
Market Cafe
Milligan's B&G
Mister A's
Newport Ave. B&G

124

Pacifica Del Mar
Peohe's
Poseidon
Prince of Wales
Quails Inn
Qwiigs B&G
Rancho Valencia
Ruby's Diner
Rusty Pelican
Sally's
San Diego Pier Cafe
Scalini
Shores
TD Hays
Tom Ham's Lighthse.
Top of the Market
Top o' the Cove
Trattoria Acqua
Trattoria Positano
Vigilucci's Pizzeria
World Famous

Parties & Private Rooms

(Any nightclub or restaurant charges less at off-times; * indicates private rooms available; best of many)

Aesop's Tables
Andiamo!!
Anthony's Star
Arrivederci
Athens Market*
Bai Yook
BANDAR*
Bayou B&G*
Belgian Lion*
Bell'agio
Bellefleur Winery*
Berta's
Big Kitchen*
Bird Rock Cafe*
Blue Point Coastal
Busalacchi's*
Cafe Champagne*
Cafe Eleven
Cafe Japengo
Cafe La Maze*
Cafe Pacifica*
Cafe Zucchero*
California Bistro
California Cafe B&G
California Cuisine*
Charlie's by the Sea*
Chateau Orleans*
Chez Loma*

Chilango's
China Inn
Chino*
Cilantros
Cindy Black's*
Cottage
Crab Catcher*
Dakota Grill*
Delicias*
de Medici
Dining Room*
El Bizcocho*
Epazote*
Field
Fio's Cucina
Fish Market*
French Gourmet
George's at the Cove*
Grant Grill*
Harbor House*
Hard Rock Cafe*
House of Munich
Hsu's Szechuwan*
Humphrey's*
Il Fornaio*
Il Forno*
Ingrid's
Italia Mia
Itri*
Jake's*
Jared's*
Juke Joint Cafe
Kaiserhof
Karinya*
Karl Strauss Brew. Gardens*
Kenny's Steak Pub*
Lael's
La Fonda
La Terrazza
Laurel
Le Fontainebleau
Liaison
Lorna's
Maharajah
Maitre D'*
Manhattan*
Marine Room
Market Cafe
Mille Fleurs*
Milligan's B&G*
Miss China
Mission Hills Café*
Mister A's*
Mixx*
Montanas Grill

Morton's*
Old Town Mexican*
Old Trieste
Olé Madrid*
150 Grand Café*
Osteria Panevino
Pacifica Del Mar*
Pacific Coast Grill*
Palenque
Parioli Italian Bistro
Parkhouse Eatery
Parrot Grill*
Peohe's
Piatti
Picoso
Pinnacle Peak*
Pisces
Pizza Bella
Planet Hollywood*
Prego*
Primavera*
Prince of Wales*
Princess Pub*
Putnam's*
Rainwater's*
Rancho Valencia*
Red Sea
Red Tracton's*
Rest. Europa
Rist. Michelangelo*
Rusty Pelican*
Ruth's Chris*
Sally's
Salvatore's*
Sammy's Pizza*
Sante*
Saska's*
Scalini*
Sevilla*
Sherman's*
Shores*
Siam*
Sirino's
Spice & Rice
St. James Bar
Sze Chuan*
Tapenade
TD Hays*
Terra*
Thai House
Tony's Jacal*
Top o' the Cove
Torreyana Grille*
Trattoria Acqua*
Trattoria Fantastica*

Trattoria La Strada
Trattoria Mannino*
Trattoria Portobello
Tutto Mare*
Venetian Rest.*
Vicino Mare*
Vivace*
When in Rome*
Yen's Wok
Zagarella*

People-Watching
Alfonso's
Arrivederci
Asti Ristorante
BANDAR
Bayou B&G
Bella Luna
Blue Point Coastal
Buffalo Joe's
Bully's
Cafe Japengo
Cafe Zucchero
Casa de Pico
Chino
Chuey's
Corvette Diner
Croce's
Dakota Grill
de Medici
Dick's Last Resort
Dobson's
Epazote
Field
Fio's Cucina
George's at the Cove
Green Flash
Gulf Coast Grill
Hamburger Mary's
Hang Ten
Hard Rock Cafe
Humphrey's
Il Forno
Itri
Jose's Courtroom
Juke Joint Cafe
Karl Strauss Brew./Grill
Kemo Sabe
La Provence
La Terrazza
Laurel
La Vache & Co.
La Valencia
Marine Room
Mexican Village

126

Mille Fleurs
Milligan's B&G
Mixx
Montanas Grill
Old Ox
Olé Madrid
Osteria Panevino
Pacifica Del Mar
Palomino Euro Bistro
Pamplemousse Grille
Paper Moon Cafe
Parrot Grill
Peohe's
P.F. Chang's
Piatti
Planet Hollywood
Poseidon
Prego
Princess Pub
Putnam's
Rancho El Nopal
Rancho Valencia
Rhinoceros Cafe
Roppongi
Royal Thai Cuisine
Sally's
Sammy's Pizza
Scalini
Seau's
Sevilla
Sirino's
Spice & Rice
Sushi on the Rock
Taka
Tapenade
Trattoria La Strada
Trattoria Portobello
Tutto Mare
Vicino Mare
Vivace
WineSellar & Brasserie
World Famous

Power Scenes

Anthony's Star
Azzura Point
Dobson's
El Bizcocho
Grant Grill
Laurel
La Valencia
Le Fontainebleau
Marine Room
Morton's
Pamplemousse Grille

Rainwater's
Ruth's Chris
St. James Bar
Tapenade
Top o' the Cove
Vivace
WineSellar & Brasserie

Prix Fixe Menus

(Call to check prices,
days and times)

Ashoka the Great
Bayou B&G
Buffalo Joe's
Cafe Eleven
Cafe Pacifica
California Bistro
Chez Loma
Cindy Black's
Crown Room
De Luca's
Dining Room
Dobson's
Field
Fifth & Hawthorne
Fish Market
HomeTown Buffet
Ida Bailey's
Karen Krasne's
La Vache & Co.
Le Fontainebleau
Liaison
Maharajah
Maitre D'
Onami
Pizza Bella
Prince of Wales
Putnam's
Rest. Europa
Rusty Pelican
Sally's
Sevilla
Sherman's
Shores
Soup Exchange
Souplantation
Star of India
Tom Ham's Lighthse.
Top o' the Cove
Torreyana Grille

Pubs/Bars/Microbreweries

Callahan's Pub
Dick's Last Resort

Downtown Johnny
Elephant Bar
Epazote
Field
Hang Ten
Hops Bistro
Jose's Courtroom
Kaiserhof
Karl Strauss Brew. Gardens
Karl Strauss Brew./Grill
Kenny's Steak Pub
La Jolla Brewing
Princess Pub
San Diego Brewing
Saska's
Trophy's

Quiet Conversation
Anthony's Star
Belgian Lion
Bernard'O
Blue Point Coastal
Busalacchi's
California Cuisine
Chez Loma
Cindy Black's
Crescent Shores
Dining Room
El Agave
El Bizcocho
Fifth & Hawthorne
Firenze Trattoria
Forever Fondue
Grant Grill
Humphrey's
Jared's
Jyoti-Bihanga
La Fonda
Lamont St. Grill
La Valencia
Le Fontainebleau
Liaison
Maitre D'
Manhattan
Mille Fleurs
Mixx
Old Trieste
150 Grand Café
Pamplemousse Grille
Parioli Italian Bistro
Peter & Harry's
Pisces
Primavera
Prince of Wales
Rainwater's

Rancho Valencia
Rist. Michelangelo
Roma Beach Caffe
Sally's
Salvatore's
Sante
Sbicca
Scalini
St. James Bar
Thee Bungalow
Top o' the Cove
Torrey Pines Cafe
Trattoria Portobello
Trattoria Positano
Tutto Mare
Vignola
Vivace
When in Rome
WineSellar & Brasserie

Reservations Essential
Asti Ristorante
Azzura Point
Bali Indonesian
BANDAR
Bayou B&G
Belgian Lion
Benihana
Cafe Pacifica
Chart House
Cilantros
Delicias
Epazote
Kemo Sabe
La Valencia
Little Russia
Maitre D'
Manhattan
Mister A's
Old Trieste
Parkhouse Eatery
Pine Hills Lodge
Rhinoceros Cafe
Roppongi
Sadaf
Sally's
Trattoria Positano
Vignola
Vivace

Romantic Spots
Amigos Seafood
Anthony's Star
Azzura Point
Baci
Belgian Lion

Hob Nob Hill (L)
Hodad's (L)
Hsu's Szechuwan (L)
Humphrey's (L)
Ichiban (L)
Il Fornaio (L)
Il Forno (L)
Ingrid's (L)
Jack & Giulio's (L)
Jake's (L)
Jasmine (L)
Jimmy Carter's Cafe (L)
Joe's Crab Shack (L)
Jyoti-Bihanga (L)
Kabul West (L)
Kaiserhof (L)
Karen Krasne's (L)
Karinya (L)
Karl Strauss Brew. Gardens (L)
Karl Strauss Brew./Grill (L)
KC's Tandoor (L)
Kobe Misono (L)
Kono's Cafe (L)
Korea House (L)
Lael's (L)
La Mesa (L)
La Scala (L)
Las Olas (L)
La Terrazza (L)
La Vache & Co. (B,L)
La Valencia (L)
Longhorn Cafe (L)
Lorna's (L)
Lotsa Pasta (L)
Maharajah (B)
Mandarin China (L)
Mandarin Garden (L)
Marine Room (L)
Market Cafe (L)
Miguel's Cocina (B,L)
Mission (L)
Mission Coffee Cup (L)
Mission Hills Café (B,L)
Noodle House (L)
Old Town Mexican (L)
Olé Madrid (L)
Osteria Panevino (L)
Pacifica Del Mar (L)
Pacific Coast Grill (L)
Palenque (L)
Panda Country (L)
Panda Inn (L)
Paper Moon Cafe (L)
Parioli Italian Bistro (L)
Parkhouse Eatery (B,L)

Pasta Pronto (L)
Peking Palace (L)
Peohe's (L)
P.F. Chang's (L)
Pho Pasteur (L)
Phuong Trang (L)
Piatti (B,L)
Picoso (L)
Pizza Bella (L)
Point Loma Seafoods (L)
Princess Pub (L)
Rancho Valencia (L)
Red Tracton's (L)
Rhinoceros Cafe (L)
Rimel's Rotisserie (L)
Royal Thai Cuisine (L)
Saffron Chicken (L)
Saffron Noodles (L)
Sally's (L)
Sammy's Pizza (L)
Saska's (L)
Sherman's (L)
Shores (L)
Spice & Rice (L)
Spices Thai Cafe (L)
Star of India (B,L)
St. Germain's Cafe (L)
Sushi on the Rock (L)
Swadee Thai (L)
Sze Chuan (L)
Tajima (L)
Taste of Thai (L)
Terra (B,L)
Thai House (L)
Tony's Jacal (L)
Top of the Market (L)
Top o' the Cove (L)
Torreyana Grille (L)
Trattoria Acqua (B)
Trattoria La Strada (L)
Trattoria Portobello (L)
Trattoria Positano (L)
Vegetarian Zone (B,L)
Vesuvio Gourmet (L)
Via Italia Trattoria (L)
Vigilucci's Pizzeria (L)
Vigilucci's Trattoria (L)
Wolfgang Puck Café (L)
World Famous (B)
Yakitori II (L)
Yen's Wok (L)

Sunday Dining – Best Bets

(B=brunch; L=lunch; D=dinner; plus all hotels and most Asians)

Arrivederci (L,D)
Ashoka the Great (L,D)
Asmara (L,D)
Baily Wine Country (B,L,D)
BANDAR(D)
Bayou B&G (B,L,D)
Bellefleur Winery (L,D)
Berta's (L,D)
Big Kitchen (L)
Bombay Exotic (L,D)
Bread & Cie. (L)
Brockton Villa (B,L,D)
Bully's (B,L,D)
Butcher Shop (L,D)
Cafe Champagne (L,D)
Cafe on Park (L)
Cafe Pacifica (L,D)
Cafe Zinc (L)
Cafe Zucchero (L,D)
California Cafe B&G (B,L,D)
Carino's (L,D)
Charlie's by the Sea (B,D)
Chart House (B,D)
Chez Loma (B,D)
Chilango's (L,D)
Chuey's (B,L,D)
Cilantros (B,L,D)
Crab Catcher (B,D)
Crest Cafe (L,D)
Daily's (L,D)
De Luca's (B,D)
D'Lish Bistro (L,D)
D.Z. Akin's (L,D)
El Agave (L,D)
El Indio Shop (L,D)
Embers Grille (L,D)
Epazote (B,L,D)
Fairouz Cafe (L,D)
Field (L,D)
Filippi's Pizza (L,D)
Fins (L,D)
Fish House (L,D)
Fish Market (B,L,D)
Forever Fondue (L,D)
French Gourmet (L)
French Mkt. Grille (L,D)
George's at the Cove (L,D)
Georgia's Greek (L,D)
Harbor House (L,D)
Hob Nob Hill (L,D)
Hodad's (L,D)

House of Munich (B,D)
Il Fornaio (B,L,D)
Il Forno (L,D)
Ingrid's (L,D)
Jack & Giulio's (L,D)
Jake's (B,D)
Joe's Crab Shack (L,D)
Kaiserhof (B,L,D)
Karen Krasne's (B,L,D)
Karl Strauss Brew. Gardens (B,L,D)
Karl Strauss Brew./Grill (L,D)
KC's Tandoor (B,L,D)
Khatoon (L,D)
Kono's Cafe (L)
La Mesa (L,D)
La Salsa (L,D)
La Scala (L,D)
Las Olas (L,D)
La Terrazza (L,D)
La Vache & Co. (B,L,D)
Living Room (B,L,D)
Longhorn Cafe (L,D)
Lorna's (L,D)
Lotsa Pasta (L,D)
Maharajah (B,D)
Marine Room (B,D)
Market Cafe (B)
Miguel's Cocina (B,D,L)
Milligan's B&G (L,D)
Mission (L,D)
Mission Coffee Cup (L)
Mission Hills Café (B,L,D)
Old Town Mexican (L,D)
Osteria Panevino (L,D)
Pacifica Del Mar (B,L,D)
Pacific Coast Grill (B,L,D)
Palenque (L,D)
Paper Moon Cafe (L,D)
Parioli Italian Bistro (B,L,D)
Parkhouse Eatery (B,L,D)
Pasta Pronto (L,D)
Peohe's (B,D)
Piatti (B,L,D)
Picoso (L,D)
Pizza Bella (L,D)
Pizza Nova (L,D)
Point Loma Seafoods (L,D)
Princess Pub (L,D)
Qwiigs B&G (B,D)
Rest. Europa (L,D)
Rhinoceros Cafe (L,D)
Rimel's Rotisserie (L,D)
Sammy's Pizza (L,D)
San Diego Chicken Pie (L,D)

Saska's (L,D)
Souplantation (L,D)
Star of India (B,L,D)
St. Germain's Cafe (L)
Terra (B,L,D)
Tony's Jacal (L,D)
Top of the Market (B,L,D)
Top o' the Cove (B,L,D)
Torrey Pines Cafe (B,D)
Trattoria Acqua (B,D)
Trattoria La Strada (L,D)
Trattoria Portobello (L,D)
Vegetarian Zone (B,L,D)
Vesuvio Gourmet (L,D)
Via Italia Trattoria (L,D)
Vigilucci's Pizzeria (L,D)
Vigilucci's Trattoria (L,D)

La Jolla Brewing
Old Venice
Olé Madrid
Parrot Grill
Seau's
Sevilla
Sushi on the Rock
World Curry

Senior Appeal

Dobson's
El Bizcocho
Gathering
Harry's Coffee Shop
Hershel's
Hob Nob Hill
HomeTown Buffet
Imperial House
John's Waffle Shop
Karen Krasne's
La Valencia
Mille Fleurs
Milton's Deli
Neiman's
Old Spaghetti
Original Pancake Hse.
Quails Inn
Samson's
San Diego Chicken Pie
Sherman's
Soup Exchange
Souplantation

Singles Scenes

Bully's
Cafe Japengo
Callahan's Pub
Cass Street B&G
Chino
Croce's
Dakota Grill
Dick's Last Resort
Field
Hang Ten
Hard Rock Cafe
Il Forno
Jose's Courtroom

Sleepers

(Good to excellent food,
but little known)
A-Dong
Andiamo!!
Ashoka the Great
Asmara
Baily Wine Country
Bai Yook
Cafe La Maze
Chino
Dao Son
Fargo's BBQ
Firenze Trattoria
Healthy Chinese
Itri
Jared's
Juke Joint Cafe
Jyoti-Bihanga
Kabul West
Katzra
Kazumi Sushi
Kiyo's
Korean Seoul Hse.
Lael's
La Fonda
La Scala
La Terrazza
L'Escale
Longhorn Cafe
Maharajah
Mandarin Garden
Market Cafe
Miss China
Mission Coffee Cup
Paper Moon Cafe
Parioli Italian Bistro
Pasta Pronto
Pho Pasteur
Phuong Trang
Picoso
Pisces
Pizza Bella
Primavera
Red Sea
Rist. Michelangelo

Siam
Sirino's
Sushi on the Rock
Swadee Thai
Sze Chuan
Tajima
Vesuvio Gourmet
Via Italia Trattoria
Vignola
Zagarella

Teflons

(Get lots of business, despite so-so food, i.e. they have other attractions that prevent criticism from sticking)

Alfonso's
Anthony's Fishette
Anthony's Fish Grotto
Banzai Cantina
Beach House
Bennigan's
B.J.'s Pizza
Blue Crab
Brigantine
Buffalo Joe's
Casa De Bandini
Casa Guadalajara
China Camp
City Deli
Corvette Diner
Croce's
Crocodile Cafe
Dick's Last Resort
Downtown Johnny
Elephant Bar
El Tecolote
El Torito
Firehouse
Gathering
Green Flash
Hard Rock Cafe
Hernandez Hideaway
HomeTown Buffet
Hops Bistro
Islands Fine Burgers
Johnny Rockets
John's Waffle Shop
Kansas City BBQ
Milton's Deli
Neiman's
94th Aero Squadron
Old Spaghetti
Olive Garden
Papachino's

Planet Hollywood
Poseidon
Quails Inn
Ruby's Diner
Samson's
Seau's
Soup Exchange
Stuart Anderson's
Su Casa
Taco Auctioneer
T.G.I. Friday's
Tom Ham's Lighthse.
Tony Roma's
Trophy's

Teenagers & Other Youthful Spirits

Benihana
Bennigan's
B.J.'s Pizza
California Pizza Kit.
Carino's
Claim Jumper
Corvette Diner
El Torito
Embers Grille
Filippi's Pizza
Hard Rock Cafe
Islands Fine Burgers
Joe's Crab Shack
Johnny Rockets
John's Waffle Shop
La Salsa
Mission
Neiman's
Oscar's
Papachino's
Pizza Bella
Pizza Nova
Pizzeria Uno
Planet Hollywood
Ruby's Diner
Sand Crab Cafe
Soup Exchange
Souplantation
T.G.I. Friday's

Visitors on Expense Accounts

Anthony's Star
Azzura Point
Belgian Lion
Blue Point Coastal
Cafe Champagne
Chart House

Crown Room
Delicias
Dining Room
Dobson's
El Bizcocho
George's at the Cove
Grant Grill
Humphrey's
Jared's
Laurel
La Valencia
Le Fontainebleau
Lobster Co.
Maitre D'
Manhattan
Marine Room
Mille Fleurs
Mister A's
Morton's
Pacifica Del Mar
Pamplemousse Grille
Peohe's
P.F. Chang's
Pisces
Prince of Wales
Rainwater's
Rancho Valencia
Red Tracton's
Ruth's Chris
Sally's
Salvatore's
Sante
Scalini
St. James Bar
Taka
Tapenade
Thee Bungalow
Top of the Market
Top o' the Cove
Torreyana Grille
Trattoria Acqua
Vivace
When in Rome
WineSellar & Brasserie

Wheelchair Access

(Most places now have
wheelchair access; call in
advance to check)

Wine/Beer Only

Adam's Ave. Grill
A-Dong
Aladdin Med. Cafe
Andiamo!!

Andres Cuban
Arrivederci
Ashoka Cuisine
Ashoka the Great
Asmara
Baily Wine Country
Bali Indonesian
BANDAR
Bangkok Thai
Belgian Lion
Bell'agio
Bellefleur Winery
Berta's
Bird Rock Cafe
B.J.'s Pizza
Bombay Exotic
Brockton Villa
Budapest Express
Cafe Athena
Cafe Champagne
Cafe India
Cafe Luna
Cafe on Park
Cafe Zucchero
California Cuisine
Carino's
Casa de Pico
Cass Street B&G
Celadon
Chateau Orleans
City Deli
Cody's
Come On In!
Cottage
Crest Cafe
Daily's
Dao Son
De Luca's
Di-Chan
D'Lish Bistro
D.Z. Akin's
El Indio Shop
Embers Grille
Fairouz Cafe
Filippi's Pizza
Fins
Forever Fondue
French Mkt. Grille
Georgia's Greek
Gumbo Pot
Healthy Chinese
Hershel's
Hob Nob Hill
Hodad's
Hong Kong

House of Munich
Imperial Mandarin
Ingrid's
Itri
Jack & Giulio's
Jimmy Carter's Cafe
Jin Sang
Kansas City BBQ
Karinya
Karl Strauss Brew. Gardens
Karl Strauss Brew./Grill
Katzra
Kazumi Sushi
KC's Tandoor
Khatoon
Khyber Pass
Korean Seoul Hse.
La Bonne Bouffe
La Bruschetta
Lader's
La Jolla Brewing
La Mesa
La Provence
La Salsa
La Scala
La Taverna
La Terrazza
La Vache & Co.
Le Bambou
Liaison
Little Tokyo
Lorna's
Lotsa Pasta
Machupicchu
Mandarin China
Mandarin Dynasty
Mission
Mission Coffee Cup
Mission Hills Café
Mr. Sushi
Newport Ave. B&G
Noodle House
Old Venice
Onami
Osteria Panevino
Palenque
Panda Country
Papachino's
Paper Moon Cafe
Parioli Italian Bistro
Parkhouse Eatery
Pasta Pronto
Peter & Harry's
Pho Pasteur
Phuong Trang

Pick Up Stix
Pizza Bella
Pizza Nova
Point Loma Seafoods
Red Sea
Rhinoceros Cafe
Rimel's Rotisserie
Roma Beach Caffe
Rubio's Baja Grill
Ruby's Diner
Sadaf
Saffron Chicken
Saffron Noodles
Sammy's Pizza
Samson's
Sand Crab Cafe
Sardina's Italian
Shien of Osaka
Siam
Soup Exchange
Souplantation
Spice & Rice
Spices Thai Cafe
Sportsmen's Seafoods
Star of India
St. Germain's Cafe
Sushi on the Rock
Sushi Ota
Swadee Thai
Sze Chuan
Taco Auctioneer
Tajima
Taste of Thai
Thaigo
Thai House
Thai Orchid
Tin Ching
Torrey Pines Cafe
Trattoria Fantastica
Trattoria Positano
Vegetarian Zone
Vesuvio Gourmet
Via Italia Trattoria
Vicino Mare
Vigilucci's Pizzeria
Vigilucci's Trattoria
WineSellar & Brasserie
World Curry
Yen's Wok
Yoshino
Yummy Maki
Zagarella

Winning Wine Lists
Anthony's Star
Azzura Point

Baily Wine Country
Belgian Lion
Bellefleur Winery
Cafe Champagne
El Bizcocho
Fio's Cucina
George's at the Cove
Grant Grill
Kensington Grill
Laurel
Le Fontainebleau
Maitre D'
Marine Room
Mille Fleurs
Mister A's
Morton's
Pacifica Del Mar
Pamplemousse Grille
Pisces
Prince of Wales
Rainwater's
Rancho Valencia
Ruth's Chris
Sally's
Salvatore's
Sante
Sirino's
Terra
Thee Bungalow
Top of the Market
Top o' the Cove
Trattoria Acqua
Tutto Mare
Vivace
When in Rome
WineSellar & Brasserie

Worth a Trip
Carlsbad
  Bellefleur Winery
  Vivace
Coronado
  Azzura Point
  Chart House
  Prince of Wales
Del Mar
  Le Bambou
  Pacifica Del Mar
Escondido
  Hernandez Hideaway
  150 Grand Café
  Sand Crab Cafe
  Sirino's

La Jolla
  Cindy Black's
  George's at the Cove
  La Valencia
  Marine Room
  Sante
  Top o' the Cove
Pine Valley
  Pine Valley Hse.
Rancho Bernardo
  Bernard'O
  El Bizcocho
Rancho Santa Fe
  Delicias
  Mille Fleurs
  Rancho Valencia
Solana Beach
  Pamplemousse Grille
  Red Tracton's
Temecula
  Baily Wine Country
  Cafe Champagne

Young Children
(Besides the normal fast-food
places; * indicates children's
menu available)
Albie's Beef Inn*
Amigos Seafood*
Andiamo!!*
Anthony's Fish Grotto*
Beach House*
Benihana*
Bennigan's*
Big Kitchen*
B.J.'s Pizza*
Blue Bird Cafe*
Blue Crab*
Boathouse*
Brigantine*
Buffalo Joe's*
Bully's*
California Bistro*
California Pizza Kit.*
Callahan's Pub*
Carino's
Casa De Bandini*
Casa de Pico*
Casa Guadalajara*
Charlie's by the Sea*
Chart House*
Chuey's*
Cilantros*
Claim Jumper*
Cody's*

Corvette Diner*
Cottage*
Crab Catcher*
Crescent Shores*
Crocodile Cafe*
Crown Room*
Dick's Last Resort*
Dining Room*
Dini's by the Sea*
D'Lish Bistro
D.Z. Akin's*
El Ranchero*
El Tecolote*
El Torito*
Embers Grille*
Epazote*
Eric's Ribs*
Fairouz Cafe
Field*
Filippi's Pizza
Firehouse*
Fish House*
Fish Market*
Fish Merchant*
Grant Grill*
Great Wall Cafe*
Guava Beach*
Harbor House*
Hard Rock Cafe*
Hernandez Hideaway*
Hershel's*
Hind Quarter*
Hob Nob Hill*
HomeTown Buffet*
Hops Bistro*
Imperial House*
Islands Fine Burgers*
Jack & Giulio's*
Jake's*
Joe's Crab Shack*
Johnny Rockets*
John's Waffle Shop
Kaiserhof*
Karl Strauss Brew. Gardens*
Karl Strauss Brew./Grill*
Kenny's Steak Pub*
Khyber Pass*
Lael's*
La Especial Norte*
La Jolla Brewing*
La Paloma*
La Salsa*
La Vache & Co.*
L'Escale*
Lorna's*

Lotsa Pasta*
Market Cafe*
Mexican Village*
Milligan's B&G*
Milton's Deli*
Mission Hills Café*
94th Aero Squadron*
Old Ox*
Old Spaghetti*
Old Town Mexican*
Olive Garden*
Onami*
On the Border*
Oscar's
Outback Steakhse.*
Pacifica Del Mar*
Pamplemousse Grille*
Papachino's*
Peohe's*
Pick Up Stix*
Pine Valley Hse.*
Pinnacle Peak*
Pizza Bella*
Pizza Nova*
Pizzeria Uno
Planet Hollywood*
Postcards*
Quails Inn*
Rancho El Nopal*
Rancho Valencia*
Rubio's Baja Grill*
Ruby's Diner*
Sammy's Pizza*
Samson's*
Sand Crab Cafe*
San Diego Brewing*
San Diego Pier Cafe*
Screens Bistro*
Seau's*
Shores*
Soup Exchange*
Souplantation*
Spoons Grill & Bar*
Sportsmen's Seafoods*
Stuart Anderson's*
Su Casa*
TD Hays*
T.G.I. Friday's*
Tony Roma's*
Tony's Jacal*
Top of the Market*
Torreyana Grille*
Trophy's*
Vesuvio Gourmet*
Vivace*
Wolfgang Puck Café*
World Famous*

NOTES

Wine Vintage Chart 1985-1997

This chart is designed to help you select wine to go with your meal. It is based on the same 0 to 30 scale used throughout this *Survey*. The ratings (prepared by our friend **Howard Stravitz**, a law professor at the University of South Carolina) reflect both the quality of the vintage and the wine's readiness for present consumption. Thus, if a wine is not fully mature or is over the hill, its rating has been reduced. We do not include 1987 or 1991 vintages because, with the exception of cabernets and '91 Northern Rhônes, those vintages are not especially recommended.

	'85	'86	'88	'89	'90	'92	'93	'94	'95	'96	'97
WHITES											
French:											
Burgundy	24	25	20	29	24	24	–	23	28	27	26
Loire Valley	–	–	–	26	25	19	22	23	24	25	23
Champagne	28	25	24	26	28	–	24	–	25	26	–
Sauternes	22	28	29	25	26	–	–	18	22	24	23
California:											
Chardonnay	–	–	–	–	–	25	24	23	26	23	22
REDS											
French:											
Bordeaux	26	27	25	28	29	19	22	24	25	24	22
Burgundy	25	–	24	27	29	23	25	22	24	25	24
Rhône	26	20	26	28	27	16	23*	23	24	22	–
Beaujolais	–	–	–	–	–	–	20	21	24	22	23
California:											
Cab./Merlot	26	26	–	21	28	26	25	27	23	24	22
Zinfandel	–	–	–	–	–	21	21	23	20	21	23
Italian:											
Tuscany	27	16	24	–	26	–	21	20	25	19	–
Piedmont	26	–	25	27	27	–	19	–	24	25	–

*Rating is only for Southern Rhône wine.

Bargain sippers take note: Some wines are reliable year in, year out, and are reasonably priced as well. These wines are best bought in the most recent vintages. They include: Alsatian Pinot Blancs, Côtes du Rhône, Muscadet, Bardolino, Valpolicella and inexpensive Spanish Rioja and California Zinfandel.